Ashis Nandy's *Exiled at Home*

Theory and Praxis

Bijay Kumar Das

ATLANTIC

PUBLISHERS & DISTRIBUTORS (P) LTD

Published by

ATLANTIC

PUBLISHERS & DISTRIBUTORS (P) LTD

7/22, Ansari Road, Darya Ganj, New Delhi-110002
Phones : +91-11-40775252, 40775214, 23273880, 23275880
Fax : +91-11-23285873
Web : www.atlanticbooks.com
E-mail : orders@atlanticbooks.com

Branch Office: Chennai
Phones : +91-44-48531784, 28291383
E-mail : chennai@atlanticbooks.com

Printed & bound in India by Atlantic Print Services

To
My Student, Anupama Chowdhury
for
her concern, devotion and erudition

***

My Daughter, Sonali
for
her achievement

Preface

Ashis Nandy is a well known social scientist. He has dived deep into Indian Psyche and Society with his wide range of reading of Sociology and Psychology. He is also well versed in Contemporary Thought. He has enriched his mind by reading Edward Said, Michel Foucault, Ranajit Guha, Benedict Anderson, Frantz Fanon, Jean-Paul Sartre, Albert Camus, George Orwell, Rudyard Kipling and above all, Mahatma Gandhi with interest. But he has an independent mind and like a true scholar he has not taken sides and analysed his subject objectively. He puts on no blinkers and puts down no shutters.

I have made an attempt to analyse his book, *Exiled at Home* as an embodiment of social criticism by examining his views on Indian nationality, culture, history, and politics of our great nation. Like the well known Indian postcolonial critics, Homi K. Bhabha and Gayatri Chakravorty Spivak, Nandy should be read as a postcolonial critic, because postcolonialism in essence is social criticism foregrounded in colonialism.

This book, *Ashis Nandy's 'Exiled at Home': Theory and Praxis* contains six chapters based on Nandy's three books from the stand point of theorizing social sciences and Indian nationalism. An appendix is included to bring the concept of Indian Culture home for the benefit of researchers of our country.

Last but not the least, I have made an attempt to show how Nandy's social criticism can be used as a tool for the analysis of Indian literature, particularly fiction. I shall feel rewarded if this book finds favour with students, researchers, and teachers of our country.

Bijay Kumar Das

Acknowledgements

Acknowledgement is due to *Journal of Literature and Aesthetics* 18: 2, July-December 2018 in which the Appendix of this book first appeared.

Bijay Kumar Das

Contents

1
Introduction

Ashis Nandy (1937-), the foremost intellectual and social thinker has his grounding in Sociology with a postgraduate degree from Nagpur University, Nagpur. He broadened his horizon of knowledge by reading Psychology, particularly Social Psychology and had decided, "to live a life of the mind". Nandy has read with interest Edward Said, Michel Foucault, Ranajit Guha, Benedict Anderson, Frantz Fanon, Jean-Paul Sartre, Albert Camus, George Orwell, Rudyard Kipling, Mahatma Gandhi and a host of other thinkers and is well-versed in Contemporary Thought. But he has not toed the line of any one of the above thinkers. He maintained his intellectual integrity with his dissent from others wherever it is necessary. No wonder, he led a life of dissent (not for the sake of dissent but for intellectual difference) and is known as a contrarian. His well-known works include, *Alternative Sciences: Creativity and Authenticity in Two Indian Scientists* (1980), *The Intimate Enemy: Loss and Recovery of Self under Colonialism* (1983), *Traditions, Tyranny and Utopias: Essays in the Politics of Awareness* (1987), *An Ambiguous Journey to the City: The Village and the Other Odd Ruins of the Self in the Indian Imagination* (2001), *The Romance of the State, and the Fate of Dissent in the Topics* (2003), *Bonfire of Creeds: The Essential Ashis Nandy* (2004), *Exiled at Home* (2005), *Time Treks: The Uncertain Future of Old and New Despotisms* (2008), and *Regimes of Narcissism, Regimes of Despair* (2013). The turning point in his life came when he joined with a fellowship the B.M. Institute in Ahmedabad. Nandy makes it clear in course of an interview to Ananya Vajpeyi and Ramin Jahanbegloo:

> I had never dreamt that I was going to be at an institution like B.M. in a city like Ahmedabad, where intellectual life itself was so peripheral and yet allowed to function autonomously and untrammelled.
>
> After I got the fellowship, for the first time I found that I could decide what I wanted to read, what I wanted to think, and what I planned to do. They had an excellent specialized library, the kind you did not easily get anywhere else. Although I was already exposed to Psychology and Social Psychology, the exposure was towards hard, positivist versions of the disciplines. Here for the first time I was exposed to critical thought and dissenting scholars, to therapeutic schools I had not even heard of and to cases that confounded famous psychoanalysts and psychiatrists. Also the dignity that was granted to young researchers was unbelievable. It was easy to decide that I wanted to live a life of the mind (330).

Nandy refers to Gandhi approvingly to show that the latter was more radical than the left in "his critique of capitalism and foundational values of the modern West world" and hence Nandy opines that "the difference between left and right did not work in the Indic Civilization" (332). Gandhi's thought of Indian society contributed a lot to the making of Nandy as a thinker and finally a social scientist. He wrote:

> The rediscovery of Gandhi during the Emergency in India also altered my concept of scholarship. So many interpretations of Gandhi came out—good, bad, and indifferent, mostly the latter. But that made one think. Was *Hind Swaraj* a classic when it came out? Or did it become a classic during the Emergency? Can a family of disparate, decentralized, unarmed movements fight a centralized, powerful state, in full control of the media and armed with press censorship, surveillance, and a well-paid band of trolls? (334).

Nandy joined the Centre for the Study of Developing Societies (CSDS), Delhi and came under the influence of Rajni Kothari, the Director of the Centre who was both a scholar and an activist.

Apart from B.M. Institute, Ahmedabad, which was sponsored by Vikram Sarabhai family, which he first joined as a research and training fellow and CSDS, Delhi, the Emergency imposed in 1975 was a strong influence on Nandy's life. Nandy was candid about it. He said:

> The Emergency was the third milestone of my intellectual life. It came nearly a decade after I joined the Centre. Before that, I was merely an academic. The Emergency made me a more open intellectual, more suspicious of inherited wisdom, and increasingly less dependent on knowledge that came from the university system. It was the time when I often said to myself: this is not the time to keep quiet. If you have something to say to a larger audience, you must also respond to those working at the grassroots, keeping in touch with those directly affected by large-scale social and political changes. Political cultural theory might come from texts, but it can also come from slums. It is an intellectual's ethical responsibility not to wait and write a voluminous, authoritative book on Emergency after twenty years for the edification of the next generation, but to intervene here and now. Most of my columns for newspaper and new magazines came from that awareness (334-35).

In course of an article titled, "Hibernating Idealism" Nandy brings the difference between, "idealism and ideology" in the following words:

> The job of politics is to dissolve idealism, often in the name of ideology and to subvert ideology, usually in the name of political realism. I can find no better example of this than a statement of Deng Xiaoping who, I am told once claimed, "The West builds capitalism for the sake of building capitalism. We build capitalism to build socialism" (*Outlook* 23 Aug. 2017, 19).

Nandy is known for his intellectual honesty and courage of conviction. He speaks out whatever he thinks and considers right based on reason and is not afraid of being isolated. His views on nationalism are crystal clear and he understands human psychology in the context of the situation prevalent in our country. He writes:

> Hatred defines our enemies. And that definition is always sharper than that of our allies. That is why all nationalisms, especially if they are state-centric, tend to be hate-based. The only exceptions are those nationalisms that defy the conventional meaning of nationalism and use it as a synonym of patriotism, a much older word that refers to a natural human sentiment called territoriality. Unlike nationalism, it is not an ideology. It is easier to mobilize people against enemies than for friends; people usually know better what they hate than what they love. A dystopia can quickly produce a monolithic wall of public opinion deaf to all isolated voices of sanity (*Outlook* 21 Aug. 2017, 20).

Nandy is of the opinion that the problems that crop up in the society and country must be highlighted and written about in the right earnest. People should not discuss the issues as an after thought long after the actual happenings are over. Thus, he says:

> This is what I learnt during the Emergency, that either you write when the chips are down or you don't write at all. What is the point of your political psychology if you cannot comment on the Emergency when it faces you right here and you are sitting in the belly of the beast? (Jahanbegloo and Vajpeyi 339).

Nandy has an open mind. His grounding in clinical psychology and indebtedness to Freudian Psychology enabled him to write numerous essays on literary history, contemporary film, religious conflict, technology, colonialism—above all, political culture in India which are useful to study and do research in social sciences, even literature. Raewyn Connell makes this clear in her book (Chapter VIII):

> He (Nandy) has a detailed knowledge of rich Indian traditions of religious, philosophical and political thought, literature and art, and makes free use of these resources in his work. He has written, for instance, a magnificent essay on Rabindranath Tagore's novels as a discourse on the changing character of nationalism and national identity and the political construction of the self (183).

Ashis Nandy has no religious bias and rejects nationalism when it is added to religion. For instance, he is neither in favour of Hindu nationalism nor Islamic nationalism. He has written on nationalism of any thought. Jinnah succeeded in breaking the nation as Nehru insisted on getting the freedom with or without Pakistan. His impatience to assume office, led to the ultimate break of the country into two parts: India and Pakistan.

Nandy is a well-read person, who knows the thinkers of the West and the East inside out. Being pragmatic he knows that ideology in South Asia is "skin deep" because it does not take the ground reality that is, what is going on around seriously. For him 'myths' are moral tales and are not based on practicality. He wrote about two well-known Indian scientists such as Jagadish Chandra Bose, the Botanist of international repute and Srinivasa Ramanujan the world acclaimed Mathematician, who has become a legend in his lifetime. No wonder, his first book was appropriately titled, *Alternative Sciences: Creativity and Authenticity in Two Indian Scientists* (1980). He also wrote two brilliant essays on Swami Vivekananda and Mahatma Gandhi explicating their ideas from the standpoint of their times. The full titles of the two articles are, "Vivekananda and Secularism: A Nineteenth Century Solution and a Twentieth Century Problem", *Quest* 81 (March-April 1973, 73-75), and "Final Encounter: The Politics of the Assassination of Gandhi", *At the Edge of Psychology: Essays in Politics and Culture* (New Delhi: OUP, 1980).

Nandy's originality lies in his insight into the problems he discusses in his essays and books, without fear and favour. Like a true scholar, he never takes sides but hits the nail in the head. For instance, in his works one notices that he does not blame the colonizer alone for what happened to Indians in the colonial era but squarely blames the educated colonized for being guilty of complicity in the process. He reminds us of the fact that with colonialism came Christianity and indigenous Brahmoism. It is a fact that many educated persons and intellectuals in Bengal, Odisha and other parts of India became Christians (most of them were converted into Christianity).

Utkal Gourav Madhusudan Das (the pride of Odisha) who was instrumental in making Orissa (then) a separate state on the linguistic basis in 1936, some twenty years before Madras and Andhra were created as separate states on the basis of language, Tamil and Telugu respectively, became a Christian. Nandy explains Vivekananda's Chicago speech as an attempt on the part of the latter to highlight Hindu religion to guard against the onslaught of Christian religion. He has opined that Vivekananda might have, "introduced the concept of hierarchy into Hindu metaphysics and the concept of equity into Hindu institutions" ("Vivekananda and Secularism" 74).

Nandy's analysis of the events and the situation prevalent in our country around the time of our Independence (1947) is both critical and scholarly. Hence, Gandhiji's assassination must be considered against the backdrop the political situation prevalent in our country. Keeping that in mind, I have made an in-depth analysis of the essay, on the assassination of Gandhi in Chapter 3 of the book. Let me cite a few lines from, "Final Encounter: The Politics of the Assassination of Gandhi":

> The first was his continuous attempt to change the definitions of centre and periphery in Indian society; the second was his negation of the concepts of masculinity and femininity implicit in some Indian traditions and in the colonial situation. Both these attempted changes had important psychological components and the drama of Gandhi's death cannot be told without reference to them (71).

Exiled at Home is a collection of three books, *At the Edge of Psychology, The Intimate Enemy,* and *Creating a Nationality*. The first book begins with "Sati Pratha" in the colonial era, and moves on to describe political culture in India, Gandhi's assassination, Indira Gandhi's politics, Indian culture, and political and cultural psychology. The second book deals with colonialism and postcolonialism. And the last book is a collaborative effort of four persons including Ashis Nandy, which deals with the making of a Nation and the Ramjanmabhumi Movement. Ashis Nandy is a social theorist who combines history, politics, sociology, psychology, and culture in his works and what he says is already in the public domain. The subject he deals with in *Exiled at Home* is not new, but the interpretation is his own. That is the hall mark of the book.

Nandy has been variously described as a political psychologist, clinical psychologist, a contrarian, a dissenter—he is all these and much more. He is also a historian, who has sound knowledge of India's contemporary history starting from Gandhi's assassination to the Ramjanmabhumi Movement and above all, Indira Gandhi's style of functioning. Here is a burning example of Indira Gandhi's way of doing things:

> Disowning this tradition of institution building, Indira Gandhi tried to take advantage of the Indian's deep-seated skepticism about the organized modern sector of the society and to make some of the major institutions of the country subservient to a small coterie of political power-holders. If this was not possible, she preferred to break the institutions and organization. So gradually all the important new institutions which stood between the rulers and the ruled—the judiciary, the trade unions, the press, the political parties including her own party and parliament—were one by one weakened or wrecked (*At the Edge of Psychology* 121).

Nandy continues:

> None the less, as Nayantara Sahgal has argued, Indira Gandhi brought into Indian politics a new awareness of 'us' and 'they', the 'us' being in essence only an extension of her own personal political interests legitimized as impersonal national interests. She tried hard to modify the language of Indian politics so that those who criticized her, by definition, became attackers of the institution of the Prime Minister and those who opposed her became irresponsible or frustrated conspirators operating from outside the boundaries of legitimate politics (*At the Edge of Psychology* 122).

Nandy dives deep into contemporary Indian society and points out how politics makes inroads into Education, Science, Cinema, and awards in various fields in recent times (mostly in post-1980s and after). Added to this is the politics of dynasty, caste, and religion, which vitiates the atmosphere of the society. Thus, he writes:

> ...everything is reduced to politics and politics intrudes into everything. Once, caste- and religion-based politics and dynastic politics were cases of primordial ties trespassing into democratic politics. Now they are part of normal politics. If you think they are parts of an unavoidable phase in a highly diverse, unequal society where political ideologies do not have much play, there is, for your entertainment, university politics (which subsumes student politics, politics of college admissions and appointment of teachers and vice chancellors, and politics of curricula); politics of science and science-bureaucrats; politics of sports and cinema, and cutting across some of these domains, awards politics till it produced an unworthy progeny called politics of returning awards, which was quickly dubbed, officially as nasty, anti-national, conspiratorial politics). Now to this long list you could add a new, colourful entrant—the politics of post-retirement benefits (*Outlook* 21 Aug. 2017, 19-20).

Awards in any field, be it Cinema, Literature and the Padma Awards have become suspect. Not that all the Awards were manipulated, and all the awardees got them by manipulation and groupism. But certainly, a large number of them fall under this category. In post-2015, there came a gang, infamously called, 'Award-wapsi gang', who under pressure have returned or threatened to return the Awards under the pretext of lack of freedom, tolerance and what not, in our country. If what they say is reported in the print and electronic media and when they are shown on the television, how can they say that their freedom is curtailed? Moreover, the literary award is given by Sahitya Akademi, an autonomous body—not by the government of the day. What is the logic behind the return of the award after the government has been changed? After all, governments come and go, and then come again to power being voted by the people of the country—that is what democracy is all about. Where is the intolerance? In August 2018 in a television interview to the

Republic Channel, Arnab Goswami, Vishwanath Prasad Tiwari, former President of the Sahitya Akademi disclosed the fact that this "award-wapsi gang" was under pressure to return the award. He also mentioned that Professor Shiv K. Kumar wrote to the Sahitya Akademi saying that he was under pressure to return his award. This incident corroborates Ashis Nandy when he says that politics has made deep inroads into society affecting all the systems in our country. Intellectuals (or so-called intellectuals) are not above it.

Nandy has closely read Gandhi, especially his *Hind Swaraj* to understand the emergence of the "new cultural iconography" in Gandhi's time, which Nandy calls 'hyper-masculinity'. This new term has been translated into Gujarati, "Chhappan Inch Ni Chhati". Now we have to understand Prime Minister Narendra Modi in this light, when he says "Chhappan Inch Ni Chhati" metaphorically meaning hyper-masculinity of a daring individual.

Nandy writes not for Indians only but for Asian, African, and Latin American audience. He says,

> I have worked for years with Asian and African scholars, perhaps a little less with South American scholars. For more than twenty-five years, I regularly went to four South Asian countries—Bangladesh, Nepal, Pakistan and Sri Lanka—and my intellectual collaborators mostly come from these countries. You can guess it from even from my references and footnotes. I have recently said in a lecture in Japan that if, following Benedict Anderson, a nation can be an imagined community, there is no reason why Asia cannot also be another kind of community with a distinct set of attributes. The same thing can be said about the Third World (Jahanbegloo and Vajpeyi 337).

In the chapters that follow I have closely examined *Exiled at Home* in the light of the theories of Social Sciences and tried to place Nandy's social criticism on the map of postcolonial criticism. In the concluding chapter I have made an attempt to show how far social criticism is helpful (or otherwise) to the interpretation of literature. In other words, let us find out if there is any scope for social theory and criticism to be a tool for the interpretation of Indian literature, particularly in the light of Jacques Derrida's innovative term 'human sciences' which combines literature and social science together.

WORKS CITED

Connell, Raewyn. *Southern Theory: The Global Dynamics of Knowledge in Social Science*. Chennai: Allen and Unwing, 2009. Print.

Jahanbegloo, Ramin and Ananya Vajpeyi, ed. *Ashis Nandy: A Life in Dissent*. New Delhi: Oxford University Press, 2018. Print.

Nandy, Ashis. *Exiled at Home*. New Delhi: Oxford University Press, 2005. Rpt. 2012. Print.

——. *At the Edge of Psychology* in *Exiled at Home*. New Delhi: Oxford University Press, 2005. Rpt. 2012. Print.

——. "Vivekananda and Secularism: A Nineteenth Century and a Twentieth Century Problem". *Quest* 81 (March-April 1973: 73-75).

——. "Hibernating Idealism", *Outlook* 57: 34 (21 August 2017). Print.

2

Theorizing Social Sciences and Nationalism

Traditionally subjects were divided into two parts: content subjects and skill subjects. Content subjects are judged on the basis of truth: right or wrong, while skill subjects are evaluated on the basis of validity. Accordingly, subjects of Natural Sciences such as Physics, Chemistry, Biology, Medicine, Agriculture, Engineering fall under the first category—that is, content subjects. Literature, on the other hand deals not with truth (i.e., right or wrong) but with validity. In between these two fall Social Sciences such as Sociology, Psychology, Anthropology, Political Science, Economics, etc. which do not deal with truth or validity alone but with both. That is because the truth they deal with is relative—not absolute, which can be argued 'for' and 'against'. For instance, we can say ten points in favour of joint-family system and an equal number of points against it. That is the nature of the subject. No wonder, E.M. Forster gives two cheers to democracy—not, three. Moreover, social sciences like literature employ metaphorical language. Hence, Jacques Derrida brought social sciences and literature under one umbrella by coining a term called "Human Sciences".

Theorizing Social Sciences in India is not an easy task—that is because the subjects have widened their horizon. Social Sciences include history, and contemporary politics, gender relationship, communal violence, and tension. Ashis Nandy's *Exiled at Home* contains all these subjects. Culture and nationality come within the purview of social sciences. Social theory includes the theory of culture and nation (nationality and nation-state). In a well-known book, *Southern Theory: The Global Dynamics of Knowledge in Social Science*, Raewyn Connell speaks of "Northern theory" and "Southern theory".

Connell states that, 'Northern Theory' examines "how modern social science embeds the viewpoints, perspectives and problems of metropolitan society, while presenting itself as universal knowledge" (VII-VIII). She goes on to say that, 'Southern theory' is about, "social theorizing that has arisen in four situations where dependence has been challenged: postcolonial Africa, modernizing Iran, Latin America since World War II and India since the Emergency of the 1970s" (VIII). Connell's statement could be extended further to include Satipratha, subaltern studies and colonial situation in India. Here I am reminded of Homi K. Bhabha's observation that, "the term postcolonial is increasingly used to describe that form of social criticism that bears witness to those unequal and uneven processes of representation by which the historical experience of once colonized Third World comes to be framed in the West" (*Critical Fictions* 63).

One of the heinous crimes perpetuated in our society was 'Satipratha' in Rajasthan, Bengal and some other parts of our country, according to which a woman was made to jump into the funeral fire of her husband. There was no option left for her. She had no voice and was treated as a subaltern. Gayatri Chakravorty Spivak's essay, "Can the Subaltern Speak?" popularized the term:

> The subaltern cannot speak. There is no virtue in global laundry lists with 'woman' as a pious item. Representation has not withered away. The female intellectual as intellectual has a circumscribed task which she must not disown with a flourish (1988: 308).
>
> 'Subaltern' means the colonized/oppressed subject whose voice has been silenced. The term has a relevance to the study of Third World countries especially to India (Das 145).

Subaltern studies is a bright example of social criticism in India. Its origin dates back to late seventies when a group of British and

Indian historians decided to launch a journal in India to espouse the cause of subaltern studies.

> Subaltern Studies began its impressive career in England at the end of the 1970s, when conversations on subaltern themes among a small group of English and Indian historians led to a proposal to launch a new journal in India. Oxford University Press in New Delhi agreed instead to publish three volumes of essays called *Subaltern Studies: Writings on South Asian History and Society*. These appeared annually from 1982 and their success stimulated three more volumes in the next five years, all edited by Ranajit Guha. When he retired as editor in 1989 Ranajit Guha and eight collaborators had written thirty-four of forty-seven essays in six Subaltern Studies volumes, as well as fifteen related books. By 1993, the group he remembers as originally being, 'an assortment of marginalized academics' had sufficient international prestige for a Latin America Subaltern Studies Group to be inspired "by this interdisciplinary organisation of South Asian scholars led by Ranajit Guha." Today, eleven (on counting) Subaltern Studies volumes have appeared. They include essays by forty-four authors whose allied publications approach two hundred, including translations in several languages, yet the core group still includes eight founders and Ranajit Guha's "intellectual driving force is still visible" (Das 146-47).

Selected Subaltern Studies (1988) edited by Ranajit Guha and Gayatri Chakravorty Spivak with a foreword by Edward Said popularized Subaltern Studies in the nineteen nineties. It is not that the inferior people were called subalterns but also 'woman' was placed in that category in the patriarchal society when they are placed on bet by their husbands, as was the case of Draupadi in *The Mahabharata*. Ashis Nandy's two essays, "Sati: A Nineteenth -Century Tale of Women, Violence and Protest" and "Woman versus Womanliness in India: An Essay in Cultural and Political Psychology" exemplify the theory of subalternity, a well-known social theory in the Indian context.

The title of Gayatri Chakravorty Spivak's essay "Can the Subaltern Speak?" is ambiguous because the speaker in question is unknown. Is he the subaltern? Or is he an imperialist or a person of the native ruling class? The language is in question because it is not known in which tongue the subaltern would speak. The elaborate theory and praxis would be dealt with in the Chapter III of this book with reference to the two above-mentioned essays by Ashis Nandy. During the British rule in India two aspects of Indian society—Patriarchy and religious outlook—came into the open. It is the male ego in India which subjugated the female and made her subservient, flared up against the British. It was time to vindicate the male ego in the Indian society. Ashis Nandy understands it well and tries to explain it in the following words:

> They (i.e., the Indians) sought to redeem the Indians' masculinity by defeating the British, often fighting against hopeless odds, to free the former once and for all from historical memory of their own humiliating defeat in violent-power play and 'tough politics' (*The Intimate Enemy* 9).

No wonder the Indian male was conscious of 'aggression', 'achievement', 'control', 'competition' and 'power'. Male voice represents anti-colonial nationalism in the Indian context.

Nandy theorizes colonisation of the Indian society. His book, *The Intimate Enemy: Loss and Recovery of Self Under Colonialism* is focused on this issue. The Binary distinction between the colonizer (i.e., England/France) and the colonized India is well portrayed in Nandy's book, *Exiled at Home*. Indigenous history and culture have been analysed by Nandy in different texts. Nandy being a clinical psychologist dives deep into Mahatma Gandhi's assassination in his well-thought out essay, "The Politics of the Assassination of Gandhi".

Three important aspects of theorization of society and social science are culture, politics, and ethics. Hence the canvas of Nandy's study is vast. Culture lies in insignificant things which go unnoticed in ordinary times. But when the occasion comes their significance is noticed by the people of the land. For example, no religious function—be it house warming, marriage, sacred thread ceremony even funeral rites can be performed in any Hindu House from Kashmir to Kanyakumari in the absence of the Ganga water. Water is the generic force and hence, rivers are sacred to us. In the Indian culture, the country is, the motherland (not the fatherland) the river is the Mother (Ganga Mata, i.e., the river Ganges), and the Himalayas are also worshipped as mother. "Bande Matram" Hail to the Motherland is ingrained in our culture. Culture is a unifying force—not a divisive force like organized religion. After the death of a renowned person his ashes are immersed in the river water, as was done in case of Jawaharlal Nehru and again in August 2018 the same honour was given to Atal Behari Vajpayee when his ashes were being immersed in different rivers of the country. This is a social practice, we may say social ethics.

In an essay, "Culture is Ordinary" (1958) Raymond Williams states clearly and unequivocally that, "culture is ordinary"; that is the first fact. He goes on to explain how human society functions in the following paragraphs:

> Every human society has its own shape, its own purposes, its own meanings. Every human society expresses these, in institutions, and in arts and learning. The making of a society is the finding of common meanings and directions, and its growth is an active debate and amendment under the pressure of experience, contact, and discovery, writing themselves into the land. The growing society is there, yet it is also made and remade in every individual mind. The making of a mind is, first, the slow learning of shapes, purposes, and meanings, so that work, observation and communication are possible. Then, second, but equal in importance, is the testing of these in experience, the making of new observations, comparisons, and meanings. A culture has two aspects: the known meanings and directions, which its members are trained to; the new observations and meanings and directions, which are offered and tested. These are the ordinary processes of human societies and human minds, and we see through them the nature of a culture: that it is always both traditional and creative;

> that it is both the most ordinary common meanings and the finest individual meanings. We use the word culture in these two senses: to mean a whole way of life—the common meanings; to mean the arts and learning—the special processes of discovery and creative effort (Badmington and Thomas 83).

All theorists of Social Sciences take into account two basic facts: how the society exists and how it functions. Since the existence and structure of society varies from place to place—for that matter from country to country social theories vary across the globe. That is the reason why Raewyn Connell divides social theory into two: Northern theory and Southern theory. India comes under Southern theory and Ashis Nandy is a southern theorist of social science who writes for Asia in general and India in particular. Basically, Nandy is a dissenter who questions the traditional norm of the Indian society and interprets it from a new angle.

India is not a monocultural country—it is a multicultural country. Kapila Vatsyayan asks a pertinent question: 'Socially, Where Were We?' and then goes on to answer:

> Socially there were many clusters, that we recognize as tribal societies. Today we call them, in the universal language of UNESCO, indigenous people. But then, does that mean all of us are not indigenous people? I have a report here on creative diversity in which they have given the names of the indigenous people of India and we use that most of the time. The moment we use this word indigenous people, we also translate that into the Adivasis, SCs, STs, OBCs, etc. I will come to that in a minute. These were not the Red Indians or the Hopis. These were not the Navahos. These were *us*. And we have a hundred and fifty years history of these societies constantly influencing whatever you call art movements, whatever you call creativity, all this came from those groups. But other than keeping them as buffers—and we know the whole history of Nagaland and the northeastern Seven Sisters—their lifestyle was not touched. The dynamics of the cultural forces continued to function (Vohra and Bhattacharya 333).

The individuals who make different societies on the basis of caste, tribe and clan come together in a city. As Vatsyayan rightly observes that, "our cities themselves are a conglomeration of villages. Peel an Indian and a village will come out" (Vohra and Bhattacharya 334).

Theorization of Social Science is done on the basis of culture, religion, language, caste, clan and finally, rural/urban divide. IDP (internally dispersed persons) as a contrast to diasporic persons come under the purview of theorization on the basis of caste, gender and clan in our society. Social theory is close to postcolonial criticism as propounded by Homi K. Bhabha in his *The Location of Culture* (1994) and Gayatri Chakravorty Spivak in her essay, "Can the Subaltern Speak?" Since social theory is weaven around the society we live in, it turns out to be a method of reading social texts. Henri Lefebvre makes it clear in his essay, "The Social Text" (1961) and Stephen Greenblatt elaborates the point in his essay "The Circulation of Social Energy". Social Text deals with the things we see in the society from landscape to the operation of societies in various fields. History, Political Science, Economics and Psychology combine to give a theory of Social Science.

Stephen Greenblatt asks a question: 'What is social energy?' and then goes on answer:

> The term implies something measurable, yet I cannot provide a convenient and reliable formula for isolating a single, stable quantum for examination. We identify *energia* only indirectly, by its effects: it is manifested in the capacity of certain verbal, aural, and visual traces to produce, shape, and organize collective physical and mental experiences. Hence it is associated with repeatable forms of pleasure and interest, with the capacity to arouse disquiet, pain, fear, the beating of the heart, pity, laughter, tension, relief, wonder. In its aesthetic modes, social energy must have a minimal predictability—enough to make simple repetitions possible—and a minimal range: enough to reach out beyond a single creator or consumer to some community, however constricted. Occasionally, and we are generally

> interested in these occasions, the predictability and range will be far greater: large numbers of men and women of different social classes and divergent beliefs will be induced to explode with laughter or weep or experience a complex blend of anxiety and exaltation (Lodge and Wood 517).

The most emotional issue in Indian society is the attitude of Indians to religion, temple, mosque, Gurdwara, Church, etc. The Ramjanmabhumi Movement in 1992 brought down Mosque at Ayodhya. It is a common knowledge that religion being sacred, is an individual's 'occupation'. Organised religion does harm to people of other faith. In recent years, we had seen the demolition of Babri Masjid. Nandy has inwardness with Indian society and therefore, his analysis of people, places, and history bear authenticity. Social theory takes into its orbit other subjects of Social Sciences such as history, politics, anthropology, economics above all sociology. Nandy's readings of Gandhi is objective and may be controversial to some extent, particularly Gandhi's feeling leading to his assassination. It is an irony of fate that Gandhi was not killed by the imperialist Britain but by the native Indian, who did it for a cause.

Theories of social science cannot overlook the theories of nationalism. Nation-State is a political concept, but 'nation' is a cultural concept. India was a 'nation' much before it became a nation-state (a western concept). John McLeod has opined that, 'the nation has become one of the most important modes of social and political organisation in the modern world and we perhaps assume that they are simply "just there"' (68). India provides the best example of what a 'nation' is, from the time immemorial. India (i.e., "Bharata Varsha") was not under one rule—several kings, and rulers ruled over different parts of "Bharata Varsha" and the people never spoke one language but several languages, even then they believed that they belonged to "one nation" because the culture was one. The same Sanskrit mantra used to be chanted in all the Hindu functions from Kashmir to Kanyakumari. Sanjay describes Bharata Varsha to Dhritarashtra in the ninth chapter "Bhishma Parva" of *The Mahabharata* in the following lines:

> The country that Sanjay describes to Dhritarashtra is not agglomerate of fragmented regions and warring tribes but a single, unified integrated land. Ganga, Sindhu, Saraswati, Godabari, Narmada, Yamuna, Gomati, Kaveri and many other rivers flow through its territory. Its provinces include Kuru-Punchal, Kalinga, Vidarbha, Kashmir, Gandhar, Dravida, Kerala, Karnataka, Chola, Konkan and Andhra. In this country both Aryans and non-Aryans live (qtd. in Gupta and Gupta 30).

Nation has been theorized in the west as having a tradition, a national flag and iconic figures who are adored by the people. Speaking of the history of the nations in Europe beginning with the eighteenth century, Hobsbawm observes that:

> ...entirely new symbols and devices came into existence as part of national movements and states, such as the national anthem (of which the British in 1740 seems to be the earliest), the national flag (still largely a variation on the French revolutionary tricolour, evolved 1790-94), or the personification of 'the nation' in symbol or image, either official, as with Marianne and Germania, or unofficial, as in the cartoon stereotypes of John Bull, the lean Yankee Uncle Sam or the 'German Michel' (Hobsbawm and Ranger 7).

John McLeod has rightly explained and elaborated the idea of 'nation' in the following words:

> The emergence of national symbols such as the flag or the national anthem are part of the 'invention of tradition' in which all nations participate: the repeated performance or rituals, events or symbols which take on an emotive and semi-sacred character for the people. Think of how the public burning of a nation's flag as a form of protest is often a highly provocative act. Such idiosyncratic and emotive symbols serve as focal points around which a large number of people gather as a single, national body. If the invention of tradition is central to the nation, then so is the narration of *history*. Nations are often underwritten by the positing of a common historical archive that enshrines the common past of a collective 'people'. The nation has

> its own historical narrative which posits and explains its origins, its individual character and the victories won in its name. In reality, there are as many different versions of history as there are narrators; but a national history makes *one* particular version of the past the only version worthy of study (70).

In addition to the glorification of the flag, people also remember national events and the leaders who shaped the destiny of the nation and honour them by celebrating on certain dates of the annual calendar. McLeod further states:

> Think about the annual commemoration of events such as Thanksgiving in America or Guy Fawkes Night in Britain. Each looks back to an occasion that is considered a defining moment in the history of the nation, the celebration of which helps cement the people's relationship with their past as well as highlight their togetherness in the present by gathering them around one emotive symbol, such as the burning of the Guy on the bonfire. Similarly, individual figures are identified as the chief actors and actresses in the story of the nation: great leaders, scientists, martyrs, writers, generals or admirals. These figures both come from the people yet stand apart from the crowd due to their extraordinary or inspirational qualities. Thus, a national history functions like a 'story of the tribe', providing the people with a sense of shared origins, a common past and a collective identity in the present (70).

Some theoreticians take nation as an idea and talk about "myth of the nation". In his well-publicized book, *Imagined Communities: Reflections on the Origins and Spread of Nationalism* (1983). Benedict Anderson states that nation is 'an imagined political community' (6), for the simple reason that "the members of even the smallest nation will never know most of their fellow members, meet them or even hear of them, yet in the minds of each lives the image of their communion" (6).

Anderson's definition of 'nation' can be easily contested. It is not "an imagined political community" but an empirical reality. Let me cite a few examples. When our athletes win medals in

International 'Meets' and our cricketers, hockey and football players win accolade abroad, we rejoice but if they become unsuccessful, we feel 'lost' and sad. We have not known them personally, nor met them nor spoken to them—yet we feel they are our very own and pray for them and above all, celebrate their victory. This feeling is not 'political' but 'national'. 'Nationalism' is in our blood and also in our subconscious mind.

Looking at Indian contemporary socio-political scene, such as the Ramjanmabhumi Movement social theorists speak in terms of secularism and communalism. Here is a paradox in the Indian context. For example, if one speaks in favour of minorities, he/she is branded as secular but if they speak in favour of the majority, they are branded as communal. One wonders 'why'? It is high time to redefine 'minority' in India. Muslims above 20 crores of population are not minorities and should not be considered as such. Sikhs, Parsis, Jains, Buddhists and Jews are minorities in India. Christians are also not minorities in India, and they are highly placed in our society. English Medium Schools (ISCE) are run by the Christians in India and they don't allow Ganesh Puja and Saraswati Puja to be celebrated in schools. Are they not prejudiced against the majority community of our country? Secularism does not mean favouring select communities. If the majority community is asked to honour the sentiments of the minority and so-called minority communities, should not the latter by asked to honour the sentiments of the former? Thus, social theorists should dive deep into the religious fabric of the country to analyse the Indian way of life. Indian society is 'inclusive'—not 'exclusive'. Ashis Nandy is well-aware of it.

Indian social theory (criticism) which Raewyn Connell lists under Southern Theory to which Partha Chatterjee and Ashis Nandy have contributed a lot, includes colonialism, indigenous social practices like "Sati" (immolation of a woman at the funeral fire of her husband), gender discrimination in the name of the practice of patriarchy and subjugation of woman and also communal violence in the name of religion. Women is doubly colonized—first by the patriarchal society and then by the British Imperialists who colonized India. British colonizers have not only ruled over India politically but also, they have imposed their language, culture and to some extent their religion, Christianity on Indians and thereby created anglo-mania and anglo-phones among the Indians. Ashis Nandy analyses this kind of social impact on Indians in his works including *Exiled at Home*. Nandy has aptly observed in *Towards a Third World Utopia* (1987) 'on how the west'.

> has also popularized a devastatingly sterile concept of autonomy and individualism which has increasingly atomized the Western individual. Many non-Western observers of the culture of the modern West...have been struck by the way contractual, competitive individualism—and the utter loneliness which flows from it—dominates the Western mass society (qtd. in Connell 189).

Nandy is critical of modernism and its impact on the society. Raewyn Connell has made a pertinent point in the following paragraph:

> In a later essay, 'Culture, Voice and Development', Nandy suggests that the ideology of modernization is entrenched in the postcolonial middle classes and in the postcolonial state, which is now—at least in the case of India and Sri Lanka—*more* developmentalist than it was at independence. And this ideology is profoundly destructive of pre-existing cultures. Not that it obliterates them; rather, development ideology selects from existing cultures those aspects that underwrite 'the psychological demands of modernity'. It reduces indigenous knowledge to 'transient counter-systems' that survive in corners, no more than minor irritants to the positive sciences linked with the developmentalist state. So victims of the development process have difficulty in findings a voice that can actually be heard (189).

The last point, I wish to make is that how social theory (criticism) can be applied to the interpretation of literature. If postcolonial criticism based on imperialism, colonialism, postcolonialism and now, neo-colonialism could be applied to the interpretation of English literature and literatures in English, then how can we exclude social criticism in India which takes anti-colonial nationalism as a fit subject for the study of literature (particularly, fiction) from being a tool for the analysis of literature? Social theorists should be read along with postcolonial critics to facilitate the understanding of the Indian mind. To conclude this chapter, I would say that Ashis Nandy is in the company of Homi K. Bhabha and Gayatri Chakravorty Spivak, so far as the interpretation of Indian English literature and Indian literature in English translation is concerned.

WORKS CITED

Bhabha, Homi K. ""Caliban Speaks to Prospero": Cultural Identity and the Crisis of Representation", *Critical Fictions*, edited by Phil Mariani, Seattle: Bay Press, 1991. Print.

Chakravorty Spivak, Gayatri. "Can the Subaltern Speak?". *Marxism and Interpretation of Literature*, edited by C. Nelson and L. Grossberg, Basing Stoke: Macmillan Education, 1988.

Connell, Raewyn. *Southern Theory: The Global Dynamics of Knowledge in Social Science.* Allen and Unwin, 2008.

Das, Bijay Kumar. *Twentieth Century Literary Criticism.* 8th ed., New Delhi: Atlantic Publishers, 2018.

Greenblatt, Stephen. "The Circulation of Social Energy". *Modern Criticism and Theory: A Reader*, edited by David Lodge and Nigel Wood, Pearson, 2007.

Gupta, R.K. and Priyalakshmi Gupta. "Towards a Concept of Indian Literature". *Indian Literature* 25:5, Sept.-Oct. 1982, pp. 28-55.

Hobsbawm, Eric. "Introduction: Inventing Tradition". *The Invention of Tradition,* edited by E. Hobsbawm and T. Ranger, Cambridge: Cambridge University Press, 1983.

Nandy, Ashis. "The Intimate Enemy". *Exiled at Home.* New Delhi: OUP, 2005.

Vatsyayan, Kapila. "Our Cultural Heritage and Identity". Looking Back: India in the Twentieth Century, edited by N.N. Vora and Sabyasachi Bhattacharya. New Delhi: National Book Trust of India, 2002, pp. 321-61.

Williams, Raymond. "Culture is Ordinary" (1958). *The Routledge Critical and Cultural Theory Reader*, edited by Neil Badmington and Julia Thomas. New York: Routledge, 2008, Indian Rpt., 2012, pp. 82-94.

3

At the Edge of Psychology (1980)

In "Preface" to *At the Edge of Psychology,* Nandy as it were, gives a clarification for including the "new incarnations of six essays" which he wrote between 1972 and 1977. He is candid in saying that he disagrees with many things contained in this book. But in his attempt to describe "Indian Political Consciousness" and may be "unconsciousness", Nandy finds these six essays as, "outlines of a cultural psychology of Indian politics" (v). According to Nandy, "Four themes run through the essays" (v). The themes include, "creation", "persistence", "remaking", "death and rebirth of political traditions" (v).

I

The first essay, "Sati: A Nineteenth-Century Tale of Women, Violence and Protest" is well written and well analysed. The opening paragraph of the essay puts "The Hindu rite" of "Sati" in its proper perspective and sets the tone of Nandy's argument and assessment of this age-old custom. It is a diachronic study of the subject through two centuries—the eighteenth and the nineteenth century till the abolition of it in 1829 by the British colonizer. Nandy rightly calls Raja Rammohun Roy, who spearheaded the Movement against "Sati Pratha" as the father of modern India.

Rituals are based on tradition and custom, may be superstition. Indian people are credulous by nature. Hence, many rituals thrive in our country. Nandy has an uncanny sense of place and time. He goes on to say that "social change then comes to mean not only changes in rites, rituals and practices, but also a changed relationship between cultural symbols and individual motives" (*Sati* 1-2). Nandy develops this essay by examining 'Sati' in historical and psychological terms and how Rammohun Roy 'subverted the rite of Sati'.

The twin objects of the essay, "Sati", for Nandy is to, "examine the culture of Sati in historical and psychological terms and show how the ritual became a battle ground between the old and the new" and secondly to "show how Rammohun Roy subverted the rite of Sati by introducing his society to alternative symbols of authority" (2) heralding modernism in colonial India. Nandy argues that "Sati" is an age-old practice of two thousand years in parts of India. Diving deep into the past, he says how a kind of legitimacy had been given to this obscurant practice:

> The earlier law-givers, such as Manu and Yajna-valkya, had only recommended a chaste life for windows; others, such as Kautilya, allowed widows to remarry under certain circumstances. It was in the second or third century A.D. that sati was first recommended in *Vishnu Dharma Samhita* and it was in medieval India that the rite began to gain a new legitimacy? (3)

The reasons of the continuance of "Sati" are manifold: religion, economy, war and the decline of Buddhism. Thus, says Nandy,

> Many reasons for the gradual legitimization of the rite are mentioned: deliberate mistranslation of the sacred texts by the Brahmans; the difficulty of protecting women in times of war, particularly in the middle ages; the decline of Buddhism and its rationalist-pacifist influence; contact with some tribal and other cognate cultures which believed that the comfort of a dead man in his after-life could be ensured by burying with him his wives, jewellery, slaves and other favourite possessions. Whatever be the reasons, the popularity of sati declined again after the middle ages. We know that by the seventeenth century the practice had become mainly voluntary and took place generally during times of war when it become difficult to protect women. In fact, by the beginning of the eighteenth century it had become a rare occurrence (3).

These are historical reasons which lead to the eighteenth-century upheaval in Bengal. Nandy speaks of Bengali Bhadralok tradition, and the rise of Brahmo Samaj as the cause of perpetuation of this "Sati Pratha" (practice) in Bengal. Thus, says Nandy,

> So while constituting about 11 per cent of the population of Bengali Hindus, the upper castes accounted for about 55 per cent of the cases of sati, whereas the lower castes, constituting 89 per cent of Bengali Hindus, contributed about 45 per cent of the victims. This 45 per cent came mainly from the upwardly mobile, Sanskritizing sectors of the lower castes (5).

Surprisingly Nandy makes no mention of "Sati" outside Bengal. Rajasthan which was infamous for this custom has been glossed over. Moreover, "women" who were compelled to commit "Sati" at the funeral pyre of their husbands have not been analysed theoretically as Gayatri Chakravorty Spivak has done. 'Women' is the "subaltern" in a patriarchal society who can't speak and thus, needs to be spoken for.

Nandy has not analysed 'woman' as a victim, a subaltern when "Sati" has been committed to save woman's honour from being defiled. It was not a voluntary action but a social obligation and a misinterpretation of religion. The perpetuation of 'Sati Pratha' (custom) has its ulterior motive of economic gain. Nandy makes an apt observation in the following lines:

> ...a large number of Bengali Brahmans did claim sacred sanctions for Sati, indeed, sati was seen by many observers of Indian society as a conspiracy of Brahmans. It went unnoticed by most of these observers that Bengali Brahmans, unlike Brahmans in some other parts of India, were not merely religious leaders and interpreters of texts, traditions and rites but major landholders and financiers who were increasingly co-opted by the colonial system (6-7).

Warren Hastings, the first Governor General of British India "attributed the increase in Sati in 1821 to the fanatic spirit roused by the divided state of feeling among the Hindus" (7). Nandy brings out the difference between Goddess Durga and Goddess

Kali, the former being worshipped and adored by all sections of the Hindu society and the latter, though worshipped widely is seen to be malevolent.

Ashis Nandy dives deep into the family history of Rammohun Roy to show his determination to understand the Sati (custom) intelligently. In a letter to Gordon included the *The Father of Modern India* (1935) edited by S.C. Chakravarti, Rammohun Roy says,

> My ancestors were Brahmins of a high order, and from time immemorial were devoted to the religious duties of their race, down to my fifth progenitor, who about one hundred and fifty years ago gave up spiritual exercises for worldly pursuits and aggrandizement. His descendants ever since followed his example (qtd. in Nandy 19).

Nandy shows how Rammohun Roy's parents who were poles apart and his three-time marriages have failed to bring peace to him. Three extracts from the essay substantiates Nandy's analysis of Rammohun Roy as an individual as well as reformer.

This essay does not deal only with Sati Pratha and the consequences of women's sacrifice. It is a piece of social history of India at a given point of time, much before India became an independent and a free lesson. This essay tangentially touched the problems of women who committed Sati, either by choice or under compulsion.

According to postcolonial theorists women are doubly marginalized: one, by the colonizers and two, by patriarchy prevalent in the colonies. Kirsten Holst Petersen and Anna Rutherford in the Foreword to their edited book, *A Double Colonization: Colonial and Post-Colonial Women's Writing* (Dangaroo 1986) have used the term 'double colonisation' 'to refer to the ways in which women have simultaneously experienced the oppression of colonization and patriarchy' (McLeod 175). McLeod goes on to state Petersen and Rutherford's point of view in the following words:

> ...Peterson and Rutherford argue that colonialism celebrates male achievement in a series of male-oriented myths such as 'mateship, the mounties, explorers, freedom

fighters, bushrangers, missionaries', while women are subject to representation in colonial discourses in ways which collude with patriarchal values. Thus the phrase 'a double colonisation' refers to the fact that women are twice colonized—by *colonialist* realities and representations, and by *patriarchal* ones too. Much postcolonial feminist criticism has attended to the representations of women created by 'double colonisation', and questioned the extent to which both postcolonial and feminist discourses offer the means to challenge these representations.

Let's consider this 'double colonisation' in more detail, because it affects women from both the colonized and colonizing cultures in various ways. In her book *Imperial Fictions: Europe's Myths of Orient* (Pandora, rev. 1994) Rana Kabbani looks at the production of the Eastern female as a figure of licentiousness, and Western heterosexual male desire, in travel writing and paintings of the 'Oriental' woman and the harem. Kabbani shows how the depiction of Eastern women in the eighteenth and nineteenth centuries objectified them as exotic creatures who epitomized and promised the assumed excessive sexual delights of the Orient. She shows how in reading these representations we must be aware of the mutually supportive processes of colonialism and patriarchy which produce Eastern women in eroticized terms. In addition, as Vron Ware explains in her book *Beyond the Pale: White Women, Racism and History* (Verso, 1992), colonial representations of white women as epitomizing the West's perceived higher moral and civil standards. Thus, as she explains, 'one of the recurring themes in the history of colonial repression is the way in which the threat of real or imagined violence towards white women became a symbol of the most dangerous form of insubordination'. You may like to consider E.M. Forster's novel *A Passage to India* (1924) in the light of this statement, particularly the expatriate British community's reaction to the alleged rape of the newly arrived Adela Quested by Dr Aziz. So patriarchal values in colonial discourses impacted upon

> both *colonized* and *colonizing* women, albeit in different ways (175-76).

It is a proven fact that male ethos has not only persisted in the colonial and postcolonial era, it has dominated the social scene. The latest being the resistance of the male chauvinism to allow women to Sabrimale temple in Kerala despite the Supreme Court verdict in favour of women in September 2018. Man has monopolized the society, woman, and the religious rites, lock, stock, and barrel.

This essay is grounded in Social Sciences. It throws a challenge to patriarchy. It is in direct line of Raewyn Connell's *Southern Theory* 1994. It has touched the practice of 'Sati' tangentially. Above all, it can be used as a tool to analyse women characters in nineteenth century Indian literature.

II

The second essay in *At the Edge of Psychology*, "Woman Versus Womanliness in India", as Nandy affirms is "an essay in cultural and political psychology". Here Nandy analyses the role and place of woman in Indian society, which is predominantly a patriarchal society. He puts the cart before the horse by retelling Bertrand Russell, who "was fond of pointing out, social ethics always lag behind private ethics" (32). Nandy refers to Sigmund Freud to, "point out the inequities associated with biological strata like age and sex" (32) between men and women. Then he goes on describing the attitude to sex on the part of man and woman. Freud's views on woman and sex are open to debate and can be easily contested. Tiresias myth, which Eliot so detexteriously builds in *The Waste Land* gives a lie to Freud by saying that between man and woman, the latter is more passionate in love.

Gender discrimination is loudly pronounced. A boy is usually preferred to a girl as the desired child of the parents. This attitude leads to cruelty against woman in the society. But as Nandy has rightly pointed out that, "man's cruelty toward woman is no match for the cruelty of woman toward woman" (34).

It is high time to say that woman does not play only one role that of the beloved/wife against the lover/husband in the society.

She is also a mother, a sister, and a daughter. Man's reverence for the mother, affection for the sister and parental love for daughter are exemplary in Indian society. Mother is placed only next to God. Hence, our country is 'motherland'—not 'fatherland', our river is 'she', the first language is 'mother tongue'—not 'father tongue'. So, the cruelty towards 'woman' as a lover is amply compensated by man's love for mother, sister and daughter.

"Feminine Principle" is always loved and respected and the "feminine principle in nature" is adored in Indian context. In the words of Nandy,

> A number of studies have found that such a society tends to emphasise the feminine principle in nature, to see nature as a mother who is irascible and unpredictable, propitiable only through a wide variety of rites and rituals. Particularly in societies where nature continues to be the dominant partner in the man-nature dyad, important themes in folklore and religious texts are often the fecundity and bounty of nature as well as her frequent denial of sustenance to men who have poor means of controlling the fickle mother and are totally dependent upon her for survival. This is certainly true of India. Though the Brahmanic tradition attempted to limit the dominance of woman in society, the pre-Aryan dominance of woman was retained in many areas of life, particularly in the symbolic system. This undeniably is a matrifocal culture in which femininity is inextricably linked with *prakriti*, or nature, and *prakriti* with *leela*, or activity (35).

Nandy goes back to the *Mahabharata* days to show how women were powerful and respected then. Perhaps, Nandy by oversight misses a rare custom called Swayamvar on the part of women of noble birth and royalty to choose their husbands from among hundreds of princes and even kings. India being predominantly an agricultural country with vast majority of the people living in villages, though this scene is fast changing in favour of urbanization after independence and more so now—thanks to I.T. revolution, still the communion with nature continues unabated. Nature is an epitome of femininity, fertility, germination and growth. Nandy has given a correct and unmistakable picture of India in the following long passage:

> ...the concept of *adya shakti*, primal or original power, is entirely feminine in India. It is the male principle in the godhead, *purusha*, that is reliable but relatively passive, weak, distant, and secondary. That is why the deities that preside over those critical sectors of life which one cannot control—such as the success of crops and the occurrence of famines (food), protection against cholera and smallpox (personal survival), and childbirth and child health (perpetuation of race)—are all motherly figures. All the more cruel rituals which are mentioned as indicators of Indian medievalism, have centered on the goddesses: sati, or the enforced ritual suicide of women after the death of their husbands; child sacrifice at Sagra Sangam; infanticide to ensure the longevity of dams, bunds, and buildings; and human sacrifice of various forms (35-36).

Women in India assume their authority in the family, first through the husband and then through the son. Thus, writes Nandy,

> For the Indian mother, on the other hand, the son is the major medium of self-expression. It is her motherhood that the traditional family values and respects; her role as wife and to a lesser extent as daughter are devalued and debased. The woman's self-respect in the traditional system is protected not through her father or husband, but through her son. It is also through the son—and for that matter on the son—that she traditionally exercises her authority. Here, thus, is a case of psycho-ecological balance. What nature and economic systems emphasise, the family and cultural systems underscore. No wonder all major social reforms and attempts at social change after the beginning of British rule have centered on woman and femininity. It is by protesting against or defying the traditional concepts of woman and womanhood that all Indian modernizers have made their point. On the other hand, all forms of conservatism and protests against modern Western encroachments on Indian society have taken shelter in and exploited the symbol of motherhood (36-37).

One thing the social science scholars overlook is that man-woman relationship is not based on antagonism. They are complementary to each other. One is incomplete without the other. The complementariness between the two genders are the high-water mark of Indian society. Lord Ram could not perform Ashwamedh Jnanjya in the absence of Sita. All the examples from *Purana*, and the epics reinforce that point of view.

As far as man-woman sex relationship is concerned, it is universal. But the difference comes from culture which varies from country to country. For instances, heterosexuality and homosexuality, androgynous (i.e., bisexual) are universal—not confined to a particular country or culture. Nandy's observation that, "the masculine fear here is that a man may fall foul of the cosmic feminine principle, that woman will betray...pollute or at least fail to protect" (37) is untenable. It is not that women betray only in India, it is universal. Moreover, there is something wrong with male psychology. For example, each man sees his mother as a goddess, sister as an angel, so also the daughter—they can do no wrong. But when it comes to his wife, he begins to suspect that she may go away with another man. The problem lies with the subconscious mind of man for which no woman is responsible.

Women were respected in the past as we find in *The Ramayana* and *The Mahabharata*. They are respected even now, though the perception has changed. There are women achievers in our society in all walks of life, though the number is not very high. Even then, the fact remains that no profession of our society and country goes unrepresented by women. We find, women teachers, doctors, engineers, scientists, writers, police, military personnel, politicians, pilots, and diplomats working in the country and abroad for the people of our country. Needless to say, we had and still have Women Judges, and Chief Ministers in our country. We had a woman Prime Minister in Mrs. Indira Gandhi who ruled India from 1966 to 1984 except for a brief period from 1977 to 1980, when Morarji Desai and Charan Singh assumed the Office of the Prime Minister. The equality between man and woman has affected the structure of English language giving rise to gender neutral language. When Indira Gandhi took over the charge of Non-Align Movement in 1982, she preferred to be designated as Chairperson of NAM—not as the President of NAM. Professor, Vice-Chancellor, Judge, Minister, Chief Minister, Prime Minister, President, Vice-President, etc. are the common designations of both the genders (man and woman).

Coming from West Bengal, Nandy knows their custom, tradition and rituals very well. Thus, he says,

> At least from Rammohun Roy to Ishwar Chandra Vidyasagar in the area of social reform, from Bankim Chandra Chatterji through Sarat Chandra Chatterji to Satyajit Ray in literature and the arts, from Vivekananda to Aurobindo in religion, womanhood as a symbol and womanliness as a subject of study have been the centerpieces of creative consciousness in different sectors of Bengali life (40).

He further states,

> Some, like Rammohun Roy and Ishwar Chandra Vidyasagar, tried to redraw the traditional definition of womanly identity, trying to introduce into it new elements drawn from reinterpreted traditions and to endogenize certain Western themes. Their own deeper ambivalence toward woman found in these efforts a personal adaptive device. I have shown elsewhere in this volume how true this was of Roy, and some of the new biographies of Vidyasagar do not leave us in much doubt on this score either. Some with mass appeal like Sarat Chandra Chatterji and Govardhanram Tripathi among writers, and Vidyasagar and Gandhi among reformers, tried to legitimize woman's wifely role in particularly and public role in general by stressing in them aspects of her motherliness (40-41).

Indians believe in "cosmic feminine principle" (38). At one level the woman is like divine Durga has the power to overpower man and crush him under her feet. At the other level there is the concept of "ardhanarishwara" or "bisexual god, associated with the deity that combines a god's grandeur with yogic asceticism namely Shiva" (38). Moreover, woman is always associated with creativity in India.

In Plato's parable, as exemplified in W.B. Yeats's poetry, man was originally double: femininity and masculinity existing side by side. Hence, there is always a desire on the part of both men and women to be united together, to make life an integrated whole. In India, among Hindus, no religious function can be performed by either a man or a woman in the absence of the spouse. Lord Ram had to perform "Aswamedha Jnanjya" by creating a "golden Sita" in the absence of Sita. This is what 'womanliness' means in India.

Man-Woman relationship is central to the understanding of human society. That is because, a man builds his house with his wife and the wife makes a home of it. Nandy has made an apt observation in the following words:

> To make the issues of emancipation of woman and equality of sexes primary, one needs a culture in which conjugality is central to male-female relationships. One seeks emancipation from and equality with one's husband and peers, not with one's son. If the conjugal relationship itself remains relatively peripheral, the issues of emancipation and equality must remain so too (41).

Oedipus Complex, a key term in Greek plays in which there is a kind of son-mother obsession as we find in Sophocles's play, *Oedipus the King* is alien to Indian imagination. Mother-son relationship is governed by filial bond not Oedipus complex in our culture.

Nandy finds it puzzling to see some women at the top of the social and intellectual border. But their percentage is very low. Societal norms for woman and man being different, man must be prevented from doing violence to woman.

In this essay, Nandy describes with insight the problems of society for woman to upbring her child. What is needed most to understand woman is not psychology but insight into human life and sixth sense. Men must understood women as they are, taking all the basic emotions of their life such as love, hate, fear, anger, jealousy and above all, the desire to be loved and admired into consideration. Only then, man and woman, the obverse and reverse of the same coin can become one and inseparable.

III

Chapter III, "The Making and Unmaking of Political Cultures in India" contains eleven sections: (i) "Culture and Political Culture", (ii) "Political Culture as Choice", (iii) "Power, Authority and Dissent", (iv) "Politics and Intellectuals", (v) "Politics and Social Hierarchy", (vi) "Public Ethics", (vii) "Politics as Self-Redefinition", (viii) "Politics as Self-Affirmation", (ix) "Politics as Autonomy Seeking", (x) "Politics as Banality", and (xi) "The Order of Change".

The opening sentence of "Culture and Political Culture" sets the tone of the essay, "The Making and Unmaking of Political Cultures in India": "All societies have traditions but only a few have traditions which are central, overpowering and vital" (Nandy 47). Nandy goes on to say that, "Indian society is organized more around its culture" (47). In the next section, "Political Culture as Choice" Nandy says that Indian Civilization is "a protean civilization" having many parts changing with time and age. Nandy goes on to bring a comparison between Gandhi and Nehru in the following sentence:

> There is much variation within a certain tradition—for example, from the intense, earnest pacifism of Gandhi, with its extremely limited application of unavoidable violence, to the apparently sanctimonious pacifism of Nehru, combining a universal humanism with national self-interest, to modern self-confident nationalism which clearly sees pacifism and non-alignment as instruments of state policy (48).

Nandy clearly errs against proportion. Nehru's 'pacifism' is embedded in "Gandhi's pacificism". Nehru is national but Gandhi is international. Nehru's appeal does not go beyond non-align movement but Gandhi's appeal is universal. Gandhi is with Henry David Thoreau and Leo Tolstoy—a source of inspiration and admiration for many great scientists, writers and leaders of the world. Nothing on earth can make Nehru equal with Gandhi, let alone surpass him.

Nandy lays stress on Indian Cultural history for the understanding of the country. In Indian system, politics is 'an amoral, ruthless statecraft' opines Nandy and further states that, "Indian society in organized more around its culture than around its politics" (48). Nandy further states that, "the concept of dharma or piety specifies different systems of ethics" (49).

Nandy states clearly that each generation has its own priorities with reference to sacred texts such as *Vedas, Upanishad* and the *Gita*. Thus, he writes:

> The sacred texts have also been used selectively by different groups at different times: the first generation of modernist reformers depended heavily on the *Vedas* and *Upanishads*; later, Gandhi and the nativists mainly drew support from the less universalist *Gita*. Such readjustments explain why politics in India often seems to underwrite the traditional cultural and social divisions (49).

Nandy makes it clear in the next section: "Power, Authority and Dissent".

Political power and the role of the society are intertwined, the former comes from the latter and the latter, though generates political power, is controlled by it. Take the case of Indian democracy. Governments come and go, depending upon the choice of the people, who live in the society. In plain language, the people elect the government and are ruled by it. Politics is neither moral nor immoral, it is amoral. It reminds us of Gandhi's "moral politics", which was in the words of Ashis Nandy "a rebellion against" "the tradition of politics" (51).

Authority and dissent go hand in hand. If the power (i.e., the government) tries to suppress dissent, Nandy contests it and tries to bring back tradition in its place. Nandy writes:

> This attempt to alter the Indian's cultural self soon created an inward-looking defensiveness, an effort to protect self-esteem, and a controversy over the extent to which the Indian political identity could be re-defined without full-scale Westernization. Borrowing from the West continued, but it had to be done covertly and only when it could be justified as a resurrection of India's past (53).

Intellectual exercises should be kept above petty politics of caste and populistic stand in a democracy. Nandy is of the opinion that "Gandhian anti-intellectualism" ignored the high culture of Indian society in the name of equality with all and sundry. In our democratic set up there is no practice of taking intellectuals into the Union Cabinet with one or two exceptions so far. Nehru took V.K. Krishna Menon into his cabinet as Defence Minister, who had to resign following defeat at the hands of the Chinese in 1962 War. P.V. Narasimha Rao took Manmohan Singh into his cabinet and made him the Finance Minister. Singh delivered as the Finance Minister and saved the country from the debt trap. In fact, Manmohan Singh would always be remembered as the Finance Minister (1991-1996)—not as the Prime Minister of India for 10 years.

Nandy is of the opinion that intellect has become suspect. What mattered is the politics based on hierarchy. In Nandy's words, "Indian culture traditionally applied the concept of hierarchy to more aspect of life than did many other cultures" (54). In democracy what matters is "the number"—not the intellect. That is why the progress is slow. Nandy makes a valid observation:

> The most creative intellectuals are often lost in government departments, frozen at their level of unimportance: influential positions within the educational systems frequently attract gifted scholars away from creative work; and worst of all, the self-esteem of persons not having political power tends to get badly damaged (55).

Nandy tells the truth, without fear, a remarkable thing to do in contemporary society. He does not have an axe to grind. His honesty and integrity are worth emulating. In the section "Public Ethics", Nandy accepts the need for probity in public life and urges that 'ethics' should be taught and enforced in our society. "Sanskritization" and "Westernization" are the two poles between which the Indian society swings. The evolution of Indian society during the colonial rule marks the creation of castes, particularly the Brahmins who not only controlled others but protected the Brahminical hegemony under the grab of religion (particularly Hindu religion). Thus, writes the author:

> When Rammohun Roy (1772-1833) began speaking about Hindus and Indians and Upanishads and Vedas, he was

> introducing concept of traditions based not on lokachara or folkways but on textual Brahmanism (58).

In the section, "Politics as Self-Affirmation", Nandy traces the growth of Hindu religious organizations under colonial rule. Two things happened simultaneously—the internalization of western norms, and the feeling of loss of self-esteem—acceptance of and protest against western culture in the late nineteenth and early twentieth century. Nandy has inwardness with the happenings in Indian society and his observations are pertinent. He says,

> The process began with the establishment by Rammohun Roy of the Atmya Sabha in 1815 and Brahmo Sabha in 1828; with the publication by him, between 1815 and 1830, of the first modern translations of the Vedas and the principal Upanishads into Bengali and English; and with the founding, again by Rammohun Roy, of a Brahmo church in 1830. For the first time, Hindu religious organizations began to function, at least theoretically, for the entire Hindu community; took into account all spheres of life, and tried to cut across the different castes, sects, orders and their regional variants (59).

Nandy, being a contrarian brings out the inherent contradictions of the Brahmo Samaj and Ramakrishna Mission with regard to the denial of caste in one hand and the enforcement of Brahmanic order on the other. No wonder, the leaders were 'blue-blooded' as far as their social origins were concerned. Nandy's references to the works of Rammohun Roy, Bankim Chandra Chatterjee reinforce his understanding of colonial Bengal in its entirety. He quotes a passage from Bankim Chandra Chatterjee, the author of the "Bande Mataram" anthem to show how the "Babu Class" created by the British has done injustice to Indian society, literature and culture. Here is the passage:

> The *babus* will be indefatigable in talk, experts in a particular foreign language, and hostile to their mother tongue.... Some highly intelligent *babus* will be born who will be unable to converse in their mother tongue. [Their]... emaciated bony legs will be skilled in escape, their weak hands will be capable of holding pens and receiving salaries,

> their soft skins will be able to withstand imported boots.... Like Vishnu they will have ten incarnations, namely clerk, teacher, Brahmo, accountant, doctor, lawyer, magistrate, landlord, editor and unemployed.... They will be Christians to missionaries, Brahmos to the Brahmo leaders, Hindus to their fathers, and atheists to the beginning Brahmins, *Babus* will consume water at home, alcohol at friends', abuses at the prostitute's and humiliation at the employer's (*Rachanabali*, Vol. II, pp. 10-12).

In the next section, "Politics as Autonomy Seeking" Nandy has rightly stated that the British has succeeded in creating an elite class in colonial India and divided the Indian society into two classes: the anglicized and the indigenous natives devoid of knowledge and power. It was left to Gandhi to organize this non-privileged class ad given them a voice and power. Thus, writes Nandy,

> If Gandhi's pragmatism and organizational skills concerned the liberals and the nativists, his saintliness attracted former dissenters from the mainstream nationalist ideology to a new nationalist consensus, negated the older idea of politics as amoral, and underwrote a concept of humane politics which may mean little to the social scientists, but which does make a difference to the quality of life in a polity (62).

In the following section, "Politics as Banality" Nandy speaks of nationalism in terms of freedom and culture. The political divide created two layers in the Indian society—the leaders and the followers. It was Gandhi who became a demi-god for Indians to follow and obey what he said.

In the concluding section, "The Order of Change", Nandy writes a meaningful sentence, "certainly the present culture of Indian politics cannot pre-empt fundamental alternations in the future" (65). He goes on to add, "In this sense, the death warrant of every political culture is written on its birth certificate" (65). This is a valid conclusion to this chapter.

IV

In the following chapter "Final Encounter" we get an assessment of Gandhi's assassination and the chain reaction to the event. Two quotations from Jawaharlal Nehru and T.K. Mahadevan given in the beginning of the chapter are an index of the politics of the Assassination of Gandhi. If Nehru spoke of the assassination as "a fitting climax to the man and to the life he had lived..." (70), T.K. Mahadevan likens Godse and Gandhi relationship to that of Kamsa and Krishna. "Arjuna never understood Krishna, the way Kamsa did...hate is infinitely more symbolic then love. Love dulls one's vision, hate sharpens it" (70). Nehru's statement is philosophical but Mahadevan's observation is fallacious, completely misleading.

V

Ashis Nandy refers to Robert Payne to drive home the point. He states,

> Robert Payne's biography of Mahatma Gandhi, perhaps more than any other writing on the subject, brings out this element of collaboration in the assassination of Gandhi. It was an assassination, Payne seems to suggest, in which apart from Gandhi and a motley group of dedicated but clumsy assassins, crucial indirect roles were played by Gandhi protectors in the Indian police and its intelligence branch, by the bureaucracy, and by important parts of India's political leadership including some of Gandhi's most dedicated followers (70).

Ashis Nandy critically analyses Gandhiji's personality without adulation and denigration. Gandhian political philosophy according to Nandy has 'two elements':

> The first was his continuous attempt to change the definitions of centre and periphery in Indian society; the second was his negation of the concepts of masculinity and femininity implicit in some Indian traditions and in the colonial situations. Both these attempted changes had important psychological components and the drama of Gandhi's death cannot be told without reference to them (71).

Gandhi noticed two important things in upper class intellectual style of functioning and casteism among Hindus—particularly the Brahmin and later the Kshatriya domination over the people belonging to other castes. English educated intellectuals were Anglicized and alienated from the majority of the people. Gandhi was not in favour of the inclination of Indian intellectuals to follow western mode of life. He also did not like the Brahmins to exploit the people of other castes because they were considered as lower castes and inferior intellectuals. He believed in equality among people—not withstanding their castes of birth.

In a similar way, Gandhi did not like women to be dominated by men and marginalized in the society. He encouraged women to take part in freedom movement and large number of women responded to his call favourably. Nandy makes a valid observation on man-woman relationship in pre-independence India. He writes:

> The Indian had always feared woman as the traditional symbol of uncertain nature and unpredictable nurture, of activity, power and aggression. In consequence, he had always feared womanhood and either abnegated femininity or defensively glorified it out of all proportion (73).

Sanskritized Indian Culture put men at a higher pedestal than women. Gandhi's fight against colonialism corroborates his fight against the onslaught on femininity and their subjugation. "He was, he seemed to argue, a counter-reformist, a revivalist, and a committed traditionalist" (75), says Ashis Nandy. He then goes to show the attitude of Gandhi and that of Nathuram Godse to the freedom of the country. Godse disliked Gandhi's emphasis on "political ethics, soul force and the moral supremacy of the oppressed over the oppressor" (83). Ashis Nandy writes about Gandhi and Godse with intuition and empathy. He says:

> Godse looked at history as a chronological sequence of 'real' events. So he saw the one thousand years of domination of India by rulers who were Muslims or Christians as a humiliation of the Hindus which had to be redressed. Gandhi, in tune with mainstream Hinduism, never cared for chronologies of past events. History to him was a contemporary myth which had to be interpreted and reinterpreted in terms of contemporary needs. The long Muslim domination of India meant nothing to him;

> in any case defeat for him was a problem for the victor, not for the defeated.

These differences account for Godse's saying:

> Gandhiji failed in his duty as the Father of the Nation. He has proved to be the Father of Pakistan. It was for this reason alone that I as a dutiful son of Mother India thought it my duty to put an end to the life of the so-called Father of the Nation who had played a very prominent part in bringing about vivisection of the country—our Motherland (83).

Ashis Nandy dwells on Nathuram Godse's family history and his relationship with Vinayak Damodar Savarkar to prove his antipathy to Gandhi. It was also rumoured that the brain behind Gandhi's assassination was somebody else—a homosexual or a womanizer. To my mind this is beside the point.

The partition of the country issued out of Hindu-Muslim distrust and the frustration that followed after independence was behind Godse's decision to assassinate Gandhi. As Nandy puts it:

> Like Gandhi, Godse considered himself a *sanatani* and, in deference to his own wishes, he was cremated according to *sanatani* rights. Yet, and in this respect too he resembled Gandhi, he said he believed in a casteless Hindu society and in a democratic polity. He was even in favour of Gandhi's attempts to mobilize the Indian Muslims for the nationalist cause by making some concessions to the Muslim leadership. Perhaps it was not an accident that Godse began his political career as a participant in a civil disobedience movement started by Gandhi and ended his political life with a speech from the witness stand which, in spite of being an attack on Gandhi, none the less revealed a grudging respect for what Gandhi had done for the country (82).

Historical happenings are always an admixture of fact and fiction—that is because things have happened but they are interpreted variously according to individual perception and ideology. Gandhi's assassination is no exception to this rule. People started interpreting the saddest thing in post-independence

India by empathising and sympathising with the personalities involved in that gruesome act. Let me cite what Ashis Nandy said:

> Jawaharlal Nehru, soon after Gandhi's death, claimed that Godse did not know what he was doing. I contend that more than any other person Godse did know. He sensed with his entire being the threat Gandhi was to the traditional lifestyle and world view of India. K.P. Karunakaran, a political scientist who has worked on Gandhi for a number of years, once lamented that only two persons in India had correctly assessed the power of Gandhi: Godse, who killed him, and G.D. Birla, India's biggest business tycoon, who gave him unconditional financial support in pre-independence India and reaped its benefits in post-independence India. I am afraid, at least in this one instance, the political scientist is more right than the political functionary. Nehru was wrong. Godse did reveal a surprisingly acute sensitivity to the changing political-psychological climate in India, by killing Gandhi. I can only add that the heightened sensitivity of Godse reflected the latent awareness of dominant sections of the Indian society of what Gandhi was doing to them. In that sense, Godse's hand was forced by the real killers of Gandhi: the anxiety-ridden, insecure, traditional elite concentrated in the urbanized, educated, partly Westernized, tertiary sector whose meaning of life Gandhian politics was taking away. Gandhi often talked about the heartlessness of the Indian literati. He paid with his life for that awareness (87).

The claims made by K.P. Karunakaran and Ashis Nandy in the passage quoted above are open to question. It is difficult to say whether anybody understood Gandhi correctly. He remains an enigma to all and his assassination paradoxically brought him martyrdom and immortality. In hindsight we understand that Gandhi was not a person to take defeat lying down. The partition of the country was not done by Jinnah alone with the support of Mountbatten and the British Government. The Congress leadership at that time was too eager to assume power, no matter if it led to the partition of the country. Gandhi who said earlier, "I can never be willing party to the vivisection.... If the Congress wishes to accept partition, it will be over my dead body". The partition came but Gandhi could not swallow the insult that was heaped upon him. To add fuel to fire, Nehru and Patel refused to give Pakistan's share. Gandhi was upset. His dream was shattered. A person who put 'Truth' and 'Non-Violence' above an individual's life, could not bear it.

Nathuram Godse's final plea in the Court is worth considering Justice Khosla puts it as follows:

> The audience was visibly and audibly moved. There was a deep silence when he ceased speaking. Many women were in tears and men were coughing and searching for their handkerchiefs. The silence was accentuated and made deeper by the sound of an occasional subdued sniff or a muffled cough.... I have...no doubt that had the audience of that day been constituted into a jury and entrusted with the task of deciding Godse's appeal, they would have brought in a verdict of 'not guilty' by an overwhelming majority (92).

What is crystal clear is that Gandhi did not want to live in post-partition of the country. If Godse has killed Gandhi for a cause, the then Government of India could not wash its hand clean, for its failure to protect Gandhi from the evil forces. Nandy makes a valid point in the following passage:

> Obviously the living Gandhi had already ceased to be a relevant figure for a large number of Indians. To some of them he had already begun to seem a threat to Hindu survival, a fanatical supporter of Muslims and, worse, one who rejected the principle of zero-sum game in politics. If not their conscious minds, their primitive selves were demanding his blood (91).

Gandhi was ignored in post-independence era. The forces which were against communal harmony took Gandhi as an obstacle on their path. Godse belongs to this camp. He took upon himself to assassinate Gandhi and wrote this to his parents by giving the example of Lord Krishna and King Sishupal. Ashis Nandy quotes Justice Khosla as cited above to say how the Gandhi assassinator,

Nathuram Godse evoked public sympathy after he made his final defence plea in the court.

Godse's plea is unacceptable. Gandhiji's action and intention are beyond question and above suspicion.

We can apply new historicist approach to resituate Gandhi in the context of socio-political situation of pre-independence India. Gandhi's civil disobedience movement, non-violent method brought a sea change in India. His contribution abides in our memory.

In the next essay, "Adorno in India: Revisiting the Psychology of Fascism", Nandy analyses authoritarian personalities from psychological point of view.

The theoretical concept is drawn from the book, *The Authoritarian Personality* (1950) by T.W. Adorno, *et al.* To Nandy it is the best book to study the mind of a fascist. Nandy explains:

> The authoritarian person, the study shows, is psychologically compartmentalized. The relations between the various levels of his kind are less fluid, their boundaries less permeable. His underlying traits in the areas of aggression, sex and dependency are also more ego-alien. There is less sublimation or socially creative modes of impulse expression. Thus the fascist is likely to be moralistic, rigid, unable to express or release his own impulses. On the one hand, this leads to a constricted fantasy life, intolerance of ambiguities, and high extraception (meaning, roughly, the rejection of imagination, emotions and—this may seem the psychologists' conspiracy against their detractors—psychological sensitivities). On the other, it promotes valuation of efficiency, constructive-ness and pragmatism above creativity, self-expression, richness of inner life and understanding (100-01).

This chapter explicates psychological theory to show how an authoritarian person conducts himself in a society. An authoritarian person becomes unsteady in personal life. Erich Fromm calls an authoritarian person, both as a sadist and masochist. Ashis Nandy as a social scientist seeks to explain the factors that go into the making of an authoritarian person. He says,

> What social forces breed such a man? The principal factor seems to be early socialization. The fascist comes from a family of repressive, disciplinarian parents. Forced into manifest submission as a child, he learns to exclude from consciousness his negative feeling against his parents. This process of exclusion contributes to his rigid defences and cognitive narrowness.... The parents of potential fascists are status conscious; they nurture a feeling in their children that whatever is helpful in climbing the social ladder is good. Frequently they themselves are marginal men, economically as well as socially (101-02).

James S. Coleman's *Foundations of Social Theory* (1990) is a highly acclaimed book. The opening sentences of the book, "A central problem in social science is that of accounting for the functioning of some kind of social system" (qtd. in Connell 29).

In all walks of life—be it, politics, industry, religious orthodoxy—we find authoritarianism ruling the roost. Nandy finds authoritarians in business and industry. He says,

> Often found in business and management, these men have a 'compulsive over-realism' which induces them to treat everything and everyone as objects to be manipulated. Doing things and getting things done are their prime concerns (103).

Nandy makes a distinction between European authoritarianism and Indian authoritarianism.

> ...compared to his Western counterpart, the Indian fascist is a relatively lonely man. He does not easily find his salvation in a collectivity. In other words, all kinds of authoritarianism in the Western world have been shown to have some association with a low faith in people and a poor sense of competence in interpersonal matters (105).

Authoritarianism can best be understood in terms of psychology than sociology. Man by nature is a self-centred person. He wants to be at the centre of everything he does. Power and money are two wings of authoritarianism. No one wants to part with anyone of them. For instance, a King will not take a 'no' from anyone. Power, physical and political or economic is the root cause of authoritarianism. All dictators are authoritarians by nature, who think they are the 'monarchs of all they survey'. This results in the grandeur of delusion.

V

The sixth and the last essay in *At the Edge of Psychology* is about Indian politics under Indira Gandhi. Nandy's remarks in the opening section is highly illuminating. He says,

> It is my contention that psychologically Indira Gandhi represents important aspects of contemporary Indian consciousness blown up to grotesqueness and her failures and successes are in some ways the failures and successes of India's civic consciousness too (112).

Nandy calls Indira Gandhi, 'a political institution', 'a product of four intellectual currents' which began in 1960s. The first intellectual current is the 'neo-nationalism' that grew as a reaction to humiliating military encounter with China in 1962. The second was the *real politik* which Indira Gandhi accepted to overcome the political situation in the late sixties and early seventies. She once said, 'My father was a saint who strayed into politics' but, 'I am a tough politician' (Sahgal 205).

Pure politics, which Indira Gandhi espoused, "creates a situation where every political activist constantly seeks to undo the others". Nandy makes a valid statement on pure politics without mincing words: "pure politics, being de-ideologized, amoral and uninformed by any compassion, invariably helps to build a political culture in which no holds are barred and the rule of the jungle prevails" (114). Nandy observes closely the way Mrs. Gandhi worked crushing everything that came in her way. Thus, writes Nandy,

> So, ovation greeted each political success of Mrs Gandhi and the more vocal sections of the Indian society, including its intelligentia, applauded as she politically finished her opponents one by one and, because pure politicians can never stop at that, began eliminating her more powerful supporters too (115).

The expulsion of Chandrasekhar from the party who later became the President of Janata Party in 1977 and later the Prime Minister of India is the brightest example of her ruthless action.

Thirdly, Indira Gandhi managed to gain the confidence of the middle-class people by promising to bring law and order in place of chaos and anarchy. Her individual style of politics encouraged favouritism and destroyed the very fabric of democracy. Indian National Congress became "Indira Congress" and psychophants like Debakant Barua, the then Congress President went on to say, 'India is Indira and Indira is India', a cruel joke on what Nehru once said, 'Gandhi (Mahatma Gandhi) is India'.

It is an irony of fate that Jawaharlal Nehru made his daughter, Indira Gandhi, the Congress President who recommended the dismissal of E.M.S. Nambrodipad's democratically elected government in Kerala. Indira Gandhi made her son, Sanjay the Youth Congress President and the all powerful person during emergency. After her assassination, the Congress Party chose Rajiv Gandhi as the Prime Minister of India. After his assassination, though briefly the power of the party went out of the Gandhi family by making Sitaram Keshari the Party President and P.V. Narasimha Rao the Prime Minister of India, again it came back to the family with Mrs. Sonia Gandhi taking over the party as the President and after a long spell she made her son, Rahul Gandhi the Party President and when he resigned after the debacle in 2019 General Election, again she took over as the President of Party. Has not Congress become a family party which would not permit any body outside the family to head the party? Is it not the travesty of truth and value in Indian politics? Or should we say that it has become the political culture of the party?

Fourthly, under Indira Gandhi, India lost its significance as a pluralistic society. In her endeavour to do so, she found no real opposition to her, she became the "monarch of all she surveyed".

Indira Gandhi assumed all the power to herself. In this context Nandy cites three examples:

> Unlike Jawaharlal Nehru who was simultaneously the official leader of the ruling party and the covert leader of the Opposition, Mrs Gandhi, long before she imposed her

> Emergency rule, had managed to affirm convincingly that she was the sole depository of power in the country (120)... Disowning this tradition of institution building, Indira Gandhi tried to take advantage of the Indian's deep seated skepticism about the organized modern sector of the society and to make some of the major institution of the country subservient to a small coterie of political power-holders. If this was not possible, she preferred to break the institutions and organization. So gradually all the important new institutions which stood between the rulers and the ruled—the judiciary, the trade unions, the press, the political parties including her own Party and Parliament—were one by one weakened or wrecked (121)... None the less, as Nayantara Sahgal has argued, Indira Gandhi brought into Indian politics a new awareness of 'us' and 'they', the 'us' being in essence only an extension of her own personal political interests legitimized as impersonal national interests. She tried hard to modify the language of Indian politics so that those who criticized her, by definition, became attackers of the institution of the prime minister and those who opposed her became irresponsible or frustrated conspirators operating from outside the boundaries of legitimate politics (122).

Nandy makes a subtle comment on Indira Gandhi as a person and politician:

> Put simply, Indira Gandhi pursued democracy equipped with her cognitive and motivational components of authoritarianism. Her values were democratic, her instincts authoritarian. This is where her ultimate historical significance lies (128).

All said and done, Indira Gandhi's achievement as a stateswoman to dismantle Pakistan in 1971 by giving more than equal's fight to Henry Kissinger and President Nixon and ultimately going beyond them is an act of bravery unparallel in the world. In a way, Bangladesh owes its creation and existence to her.

Out of the six essays included in *At the Edge of Psychology*, two essays on Gandhi and Indira Gandhi stand out as they give an evidence to Nandy's insight into human nature. He has the courage of conviction to write about the two towering personalities of the twentieth century—Mahatma Gandhi and Indira Gandhi objectively without fear. When other social scientists hesitate to write about contemporary political personalities, Nandy makes a bold attempt to analyse the minds of both the statesman and stateswoman of our country. That is what makes the book, *At the Edge of Psychology* highly readable and illuminating.

WORKS CITED

Chatterjee, Bankim Chandra. *Babu* (1873). Rachanabali, Vol. 2, pp. 10-12.

Coleman, James S. *Foundations of Social Theory*. Cambridge: Harvard University Press, 1990.

Connell, Raewyn. *Southern Theory: The Global Dynamics of Knowledge in Social Science*. Allen and Unwin, 2008.

Nandy, Ashis. *At the Edge of Psychology*. New Delhi: Oxford University Press, 2005.

Sahgal, Nayantara. "The Making of Mrs. Gandhi", *South Asian Review*, 8 April 1975.

4

The Intimate Enemy (1983)

The Intimate Enemy with a subtitle, "Loss and Recovery of Self under Colonialism" contains two chapters titled, (1) "The Psychology of Colonialism: Sex, Age and Ideology in British India" and (2) "The Uncolonized Mind: A Postcolonial View of India and the West" published earlier on different occasions. This book is included as a part of a trilogy *Exiled at Home* in 1998 and later reissued by Oxford India Paperback (2005).

In the 'Preface' to *The Intimate Enemy,* Ashis Nandy states the way colonialism would affect the world by borrowing the idea from Karl Marx:

> Like the 'hideous heathen god who refused to drink nectar except from the skulls of murdered men', Karl Marx felt, history would produce out of oppression, violence and cultural dislocation not merely new technological and social forces but also a new social consciousness in Asia and Africa. It would be critical in the sense in which the Western tradition of social criticism—from Vico to Marx—had been critical and it would be rational in the sense in which post-Cartesian Europe had been rational. It is thus that the ahistorical primitives would one day, the expectation went, learn to see themselves as masters of nature and, hence, as masters of their own fate (v).

Colonialism has two players—the colonizer and the colonized. They not only act on one another but there are many reversible reactions between them. Nandy dives deep into the making as well as existence of colonialism and observes:

> This colonialism colonizes minds in addition to bodies and it releases forces within the colonized societies to

> alter their cultural priorities once for all. In the process, it helps generalize the concept of the modern West from a geographical and temporal entity to a psychological category. The West is now everywhere, within the West and outside; in structures and in minds (vii).

To drive home his point, Nandy argues:

> Let us not forget that the most violent denunciation of the West produced by Frantz Fanon is written in the elegant style of a Jean-Paul Sartre. The West has not merely produced modern colonialism, it informs most interpretations of colonialism. It colours even this interpretation of interpretation (viii).

This book, Nandy states, "is primarily an enquiry into the psychological structures and cultural forces which supported or resisted the culture of colonialism in British India" (x).

Terms like 'orientalism', 'imperialism', 'colonialism' and 'post-colonialism' are interrelated. The advancement of science in the West gave them the feeling that they are superior to the East. Science and economy are two potent weapons in the hands of the West which make them think that they are far ahead of the East. Hence, comes a desire in their heart to subjugate the East. Colonialism is hydra-headed. It could be analysed politically (which is usually done) socially (i.e., how it affected the socio-cultural fabric of the colonized) and psychologically (i.e., colonialism as a mindset of the colonizer). The essay, "The Psychology of Colonialism" contains eight sections, the last and shortest section being as it were, a brief summing up of what Nandy aimed at and may be achieved in this long essay.

Part-I
The Psychology of Colonialism: Sex, Age and Ideology in British India

In Section I of the above-mentioned essay, Nandy states that the dichotomy between politics and culture created codes which affected the rulers (colonizers) and also the ruled (colonized). He goes on to say, "I have in mind not only the overt Appolonial codes of Western liberalism that have often motivated the elites of the colonized societies but also their covert Dionysian counterparts in the concepts of state craft, everyday politics, effective political methods and utopias which have guided revolutionary movements against colonialism" (3-4). Nandy like Indian elites sees the virtue of order, rationality modernity in the West (i.e., with the colonizers) and irrationality sporadic violence and illogicality in the East (India). We would do well to remember that what holds good for the German Philosopher, Friedrich Nietzsche in challenging the Greek culture as ordered and serene in his work, *The Birth of Tragedy* (1872) (English translation of the German title, *Die Geburt der Tragodie*) does not hold good for 'colonisation' having two binary opposites—'coloniser' and 'colonized' which are governed by both overt and covert political motives and economic exploitation. Colonisation was a direct affront on indigenous culture and rituals. It did both good and bad to the Indian society.

With colonization came the colonizers' notion of love, and sex and made inroads into the colonized's social and ethical behaviour. Referring to the early years of British rule in India (say, between 1757 and 1830), Nandy writes:

> Most Britons in India lived like Indians at home and in the office, wore Indian dress, and observed Indian customs and religious practices. A large number of them married Indian women, offered *puja* to Indian gods and goddesses, and lived in fear and awe of the magical powers of the Brahmans (5).

This is an untenable statement and has no solid basis to gain acceptance. On the contrary Indians have slowly but steadily took to wearing British dress, and adopting British formal culture. Two pages after Nandy makes another statement which says,

> The Raj saw Indians as crypto-barbarians who needed to further civilize themselves. It saw British rule as an agent of progress and as a mission. Many Indians in turn saw their salvation in becoming more like the British, in the friendship or enmity (7).

Which of the above two statements is true? It needs no guessing.

There are hints about hidden homo-erotic relationship between the British and the Indian men and the idea that 'white women in India were generally more exclusive and racist because they unconsciously saw themselves as the sexual competitors of Indian men' are far fetched.

Nandy's statement towards the end of Section II that, "colonialism minus a civilizational mission is no colonialism at all. It handicaps the colonizer much more than it handicaps the colonized" (11). This is an astounding statement. Nandy seems to be an apologist for the British colonizers, who wanted to do some good things by way of establishing schools, colleges and introducing postal system and railways, but behind these so-called benevolent actions lied hidden the desire to convert native Indians to Christianity. Clearly the colonizers had an axe to grind. In the beginning of Section III, Nandy tells us about the background of the colonizers in the following words:

> Colonizers, as we have known them in the last two centuries, came from complex societies with heterogenous cultural and ethical traditions...it is by underplaying some aspects of their culture and overplaying others that they built the legitimacy for colonialism (12).

Nandy quotes Marx to underplay Indian civilization and give some kind of legitimacy to colonialism:

> India to him (Marx) always remained a country of 'small semi-barbarian, semi-civilized communities', which 'restricted the human mind within the smallest possible compass, making it the unresisting tool of superstition' and where the peasants lived their 'undignified, stagnant and vegetative life'. 'These little communities', Marx argued, '... brought about a brutalizing worship of nature exhibiting its degradation in the fact that man, the sovereign of nature, fell down on his knees in the adoration of *Kanuman* [sic], monkey, and *Sabbala*, cow.' It followed, according to Marx, that 'whatever may have been the crime of England she was the unconscious tool of history'. Such a view was bound to contribute handsomely—even if inadvertently—to the racist world view of ethnocentrism that underlay colonialism (12-13).

Marx's attribute to India as a country of 'small semi-barbarian, semi-civilized communities' springs from his lack of knowledge of India's rich culture and literature of the Vedic and Puranic days—particularly the two jewels *The Ramayana* and *The Mahabharata*, the epitome of Indian culture.

Four pages after the above-mentioned quotations, Nandy refers to V.G. Kiernan to say that 'the ideological problem of British colonialism in India' was that it, "could not easily grapple with the fact that India had a civilization, however strange by European standards" (17). Who should we take seriously Marx or Kiernan?

Nandy then went on to bring out another controversy by distancing the glorious India of the past from the colonial India, which is based on half-truth. He writes:

> The colonial ideology handled the problem in two mutually inconsistent ways. Firstly, it postulated a clear disjunction between India's past and its present. The civilized India was in the bygone past; now it was dead and 'museumized'. The present India, the argument went, was only nominally related to its history; it was India only to the extent it was a senile, decrepit version of her once-youthful, creative self. As a popular myth would have it, Max Muller, for the all his pioneering work in Indology and love for India, forbade his students to visit India; to him, the India that was living was not the true India and the India that was true had to be but dead (17).

The British colonizers in order to build their colony in India tried to modernize it and revamp the education system (*Minutes* of Macaulay, 1835) by introducing English language as the medium of instruction.

It would be unfair to say that the British colonizers have done only harm and no good to India. Unwittingly by giving us their language (i.e., English) they opened new vistas for Indians to move to the world. Apart from judiciary, railways, postal system which benefited Indians, it is the English language that enabled Indians to come on par with Britons and Europeans. All our national leaders and freedom fighters like Gandhiji, Nehru,

Patel, Sri Aurobindo, B.R. Ambedkar, and host of others (the list is endless) gained confidence to speak to the world in English, a language which we have made our own. Rajaji went on to say, "English language is goddess Saraswati's gift to us". Now English is no less ours, for it is primarily being an Englishman's or an American's.

IV

In this section the emphasis is laid on cultural reinterpretation of traditional Indian mythological texts at the hands of a few nineteenth century enlightened persons mostly from Bengal. Michael Madhusudan Dutt (1824-73) who was a convert to Christianity, according to Ashis Nandy, 'declared that he cared only "a pin's head for Hinduism"—first wanted to make his mark in English literature' (19), finally returned to his mother tongue to write his magnum opus, *Meghnadvadh Kavya. Meghnadvadh* is a reinterpretation of the great Valmiki epic *The Ramayana.* As Ashis Nandy says,

> ...*Meghnadvadh* retells the Ramayana, turning the traditionally sacred figures of Rama and Laksmana into weak-kneed, passive-aggressive, feminine villains and the demons Ravana and his son Meghnad into majestic, masculine, modern heroes. It interprets the encounter between Rama and Ravana as a political battle, with morality on the side of the demons. The epic ends with the venal gods defeating and killing the courageous, proud, achievement-oriented, competitive, efficient, technologically superior, 'sporting' demons symbolized by Meghnad (19).

This kind of interpretation is done with a motive—that is, to please colonial masters.

If Madhusudan Dutt made an attempt to negatively re-interpret *The Ramayana*, Bankim Chandra Chatterjee sought to re-interpret Krishna in the context of *The Mahabharata*. His novel, *Anandamath* is a milestone in Bengali literature in the nineteenth century.

Swami Dayanand Saraswati (1824-83) and Swami Vivekananda (1863-1902) made an attempt to salvage Hinduism from the onslaught of Christianity. In Nandy's words, "They also took the position that the Hindus had been great—which meant, in their terms, Virile and adult—in ancient times and had fallen on bad days because of their loss of contact with textual Brahminism and true Ksatriyahood" (24). Surprisingly Nandy makes no mention of Swami Vivekananda's Chicago speech. That is why he says, "Vivekananda and Dayanand too tried to Christianize Hinduism" (24). Swami Vivekananda's Chicago address began with "Brothers and Sisters of America". Is it Christianizing Hinduism or the opposite?

Nandy speaks of 'the second model of Critical Hinduism' (26) and mentions the names of Vinayak D. Savarkar and Subhas Chandra Bose in this context. This kind of allusion is not only far fetched but highly misleading. Savarkar has something to do with Hinduism but not Subhas Chandra Bose. Bose was a polestar that dwelt apart.

Raja Rammohun Roy (1772-1833) was the harbinger of Indian modernism, a social reformer par excellence. He espoused the cause of woman emancipation. Like Rammohun Roy, Ishwar Chandra Vidyasagar was a learned person more concerned with anti-colonialism and social reform than with religion.

The change that ushered in the nineteenth century in response to colonialism was mostly articulated by the great thinkers and writers like Rammohun Roy, Swami Vivekananda, Swami Dayanand Saraswati and Bankim Chandra Chatterjee.

Section V begins with two important quotations from two learned scholars which dive deep into the psychology of colonialism:

> The problem of colonization did not only concern the overseas countries. The process of decolonization—which is in any case far from complete in those countries—is also under way at home, in our schools, in female demands for equality, in the education of small children and in many other fields.... If certain cultures prove capable of destroying others...the destruction forces brought forth by these cultures also act internally....
>
> O. Mannoni

> The colonizer, who in order to ease his conscience gets into the habit of seeing the other man as an animal, accustoms himself to treating him like an animal, and tends objectively to transform himself into an animal.... They thought they were only slaughtering Indians, or Hindus, or South Sea Islanders, or Africans. They have in fact overthrown, one after another, the ramparts behind which European civilization could have developed freely.
>
> Aime Cesaire (qtd. in Nandy 29-30)

Ashis Nandy speaks of economic consequences of colonialism and very rightly observes:

> Colonialism...is the name of political economy which ensures a one way flow of benefits, the subjects being the perpetual losers in a zero-sum game and the rulers the beneficiaries (31).

Many of the observations on the impact of colonialism on India is in the public domain. Here is one such example:

> The impact of colonialism on India was deep. The economic exploitation, psychological uprooting and cultural disruption it caused were tremendous (Nandy 31).

Colonialism too affected the colonizers—that is, the British people. They have what E.M. Forster observed, 'the undeveloped heart' which separated them not merely only from Indians but also from each other' (Nandy 33-34). The British colonizers were clearly on the exploitation mood—economically, socially as well as religiously. Richard Congreve, the Bishop of Oxford and Lord John Russel who became the Prime Minister of British claimed that it was God who gave Indians to the British needed to 'partake the blessings of Christianity' (qtd. in Nandy 34).

Some writers and well-meaning persons from Britain were against colonial exploitation. Nandy observes: Nevertheless... with colonialism:

> Well-known critic, Richard Ellmann has rightly stated that "The one duty we owe to history is to rewrite it" (Nandy 45). Very true. C.F. Andrews was in the company of Orwell and Kipling and was also close to Rabindranath Tagore and Mahatma Gandhi. Nandy opines that, "when Gandhi

described him as an Indian at heart and a true Englishman, it remained unstated that it was by being a true Englishman that Andrews became an Indian" (48). It remains to be said that colonized India had her sympathizers and friends in well-meaning Britons of the day.

VI

In the context of British colonialism in India, Mahatma Gandhi stands as the true representative of India and also as the symbol of anti-colonial nationalism. As Ashis Nandy rightly observes:

> Gandhi's authenticity as an Indian should not blind us to the way his idiom cut across the cultural barriers between Britain and India, and Christianity and Hinduism. Albeit a non-Westerner, Gandhi always tried to be a living symbol of the other West. Not only did he sense and 'use' the fundamental predicament of British culture caught in the hinges of imperial responsibility and subjecthood in victory, but he implicitly defined his ultimate goal as the liberation of the British from the history and psychology of British colonialism. The moral and cultural superiority of the oppressed was not an empty slogan to him (48-49).

Mahatma Gandhi's youthful years in South Africa, his fight against British imperialism to safeguard the interest of Indians there brought him closer to the understanding of humanity at large cutting across religions. He read the *Bible*, the *Koran* and the *Bhagvad Gita,* the guiding star of his life and developed a world view of life surpassing the narrowness of any particular religion. He came closer to C.F. Andrews but resisted the temptation to become a Christian. Nandy makes an apt observation in the following words:

> ...Gandhi's partiality for some of the Christian hymns and Biblical texts was more than the symbolic gesture of a Hindu towards a minority religion in India. It was also an affirmation that, at one plane, some of the recessive elements of Christianity were perfectly congruent with elements of Hindu and Buddhist world views and that the battle he was fighting for the minds of men was actually

> a universal battle to rediscover the softer side of human nature, the so-called non-masculine self of man relegated to the forgotten zones of the Western self-concept (49).

Gandhi's borrowing of 'Civil Disobedience' and 'Satyagraha' from David Thoreau and his indebtedness to John Ruskin's *Unto This Last* and to Leo Tolstoy are understandable. But it is difficult to say, from where did he borrow his idea of non-violence. Is it from Indian culture or from the Sermon on the Mount? As Nandy puts it:

> In the 150 years of British rule prior to Gandhi, no significant social reformer or political leader had tried to give centrality to non-violence as a major Hindu or Indian virtue. The closest any one came to it was Rammohun Roy, with his concept of 'daya' or mercy (51).

It would be grossly unfair to say that Gandhi was fighting for the Hindus, he always took the Muslims in South Africa into confidence. Gandhi was for India, an inclusive India comprising people of all faiths. Gandhi was also for woman emancipation. No wonder he encouraged women to join Salt Movement and Indian freedom struggle. Nandy understood it and implemented it in letter and spirit. Herein comes his apt observation:

> ...the concept of *naritva*, so repeatedly stressed by Gandhi nearly fifty years before the woman's liberation movement began, represented more than the dominant Western definition of womanhood. It included some traditional meanings of womanhood in India, such as the belief in a closer conjunction between power, activism and femininity than between power, activism and masculinity. It also implied the belief that the feminine principle is a more powerful, dangerous and uncontrollable principle in the cosmos than the male principle (53-54).

Gandhi was for United India, and an inclusive India of all faiths. He was ahead of all the leaders who sought to bring independence to India. Gandhi espoused the cause for women and brought them to public life. He became the undisputed leader of Congress and everybody looked for his guidance at the time of crisis. But it was an irony of fate that as the time of Independence came near, Gandhi was not obeyed by his own followers, though they respected him.

Gandhi is still in focus in this section. Nandy says that Gandhi preferred mythology to history. According to him, "the diachronic relationships of history are mirrored in the synchronic relationship of myths and are fully reproducible from the latter if the rules of transformation are known" (57). Gandhi is right, Myths are deeply entrenched in the blood of the people, while history is 'skin deep'. About history, Richard Ellmann said very rightly, 'we need to re-write it' and I would like to add by saying, 'we need to re-think about it'. India lost its sense of dignity under long colonial rule and therefore, Gandhi wanted to give a new lease of life to Indians' sense of dignity. Past is always associated with memory and desire is ingrained in the future. And the present is suspended between the past and the future. Hence, Nandy aptly quotes Eliot's opening lines from "Burnt Norton" (*Four Quartets*):

> Time present and time past
> Are both perhaps present in time future
> And time future is contained in time past
> If all time is eternally present
> All time is [un]redeemable (Nandy 58).

Nandy goes along with Jurgen Habermas, who uses the expression "future-oriented memories to describe the means through which one breaks the power of the past over the present" (58). That is the reason why Nandy thinks that time is redeemable and puts 'un' in the bracket in the last line of the above quotation.

Nandy overlooks the concluding three lines of the same section of "Burnt Norton" which run as follows:

> Time past and time future
> What might have been and what has been
> Point to one end, which is always present

The reason why Gandhi prefers myths to history is simplified by Nandy in the following passage:

> Gandhi implicitly assumed that history or *itihasa* was one-way traffic, a set of myths about past time or the *atit*, built up as independent variables which limit human options and pre-empt human futures. Myths, on the other hand, allow one access to the processes which constitute history at the level of the here-and-the-now. Consciously acknowledged as the core of a culture, they widen instead of restricting human choices (59).

'Present time' is the burden on mankind to mitigate history and human sufferings. It is through 'self-control' and 'self-realization', which Gandhiji learnt from Thoreau and Tolstoy, came his, "concept of free India, his solution to racial, caste and inter-religious conflicts and his concepts of human dignity..." And very aptly Nandy concludes this section:

> If the past does not bind social consciousness and the future begins here, the present is the 'historical' moment, the permanent yet shifting point of crisis and the time for choice. One can either call it an Oriental version of the concept of permanent revolution or a practical extension of the mystical concept of timeless time in some Asiatic traditions.
>
> With this, Gandhi rounded up this critique of the colonial consciousness and proceeded to fight the organized aspects of colonialism (62-63).

VIII

The concluding section of the essay is free from controversy. We can easily agree with Nandy when he says:

> I started with the proposition that colonialism is first of all a matter of consciousness and needs to be defeated ultimately in the minds of men. In the rest of this essay I have tried to identify two major psychological differences which gave structure to the ideology of colonialism in India under British rule and to show how these principles related the colonial culture to the subject community, and ensured the survival of colonialism in the minds of men. I have also, I hope, shown that the liberation ultimately had to begin from the colonized and end with the colonizers.

> As Gandhi was to so clearly formulate through his own life, freedom is indivisible, not only in the popular sense that the oppressed of the world are one but also in the unpopular sense that the oppressor too is caught in the culture of oppression (63).

The last sentence, "As Gandhi so effortlessly demonstrated for those seeking liberation, history can sometimes be made to follow from myths" (63) firmly establishes Gandhi's idea of 'myth' being in a higher order than 'history'.

Part-II
The Uncolonized Mind: A Post-Colonial View India and the West

I

This text seeks to probe into the mind of Rudyard Kipling, Sri Aurobindo and to some extent Mahatma Gandhi. Though Kipling, was born in India and spent some years of his early life (including childhood) in our country, he was an English man. No doubt, he had seen both the worlds of India and Britain but there is no reason to believe that his mind should have been colonized. Nandy seems to say that, since Kipling spent his childhood in India with Indians in their atmosphere, he should have behaved like an Indian. The opening of the Section I of the essay raises a few searching questions but the answer was left unsaid in 'hints and guesses'. This is how the essay begins:

> Rudyard Kipling (1862-1936) thought he knew which side of the great divide between imperial Britain and subject India he stood. He was certain that to be ruled by Britain was India's right; to rule India was Britain's duty. He was also certain that, as one with a knowledge of both their cultures, he had the responsibility to define both the right and the duty. But is it the whole story? Or is it the last line of a story which began years ago, in Kipling's childhood in India? (64)

Kipling who, "thought, felt and dreamt in Hindustani, mainly communicated with Indians and even looked like an Indian boy" (64) was sent away, 'with his sister to South sea in England, to one Aunt Rosa for education and 'up keep' (65). This was painful to Kipling as he "remained in England a conspicuous bicultural Sahib, the English Counterpart of the type he was to later despise, the bicultural Indian Babu" (Nandy 67).

I think to include Kipling in a chapter, "The Uncolonized Mind" is beside the point. Similarly, Nandy's mention of Nirad C. Chaudhuri and V.S. Naipaul in this chapter as critics of India can also be taken as beside the point because their mind was deeply colonized.

About India's position vis-à-vis British colonialism is ambivalent. India of the intellect is a shadow of British, which we have not been able to overcome till today. The armchair intellectuals of India still have a colonized sub-conscious mind, who think everything western is good. On the other hand, India of indigenous culture interrogates the British attitude to Indians with an air of superiority.

Sri Aurobindo fits into this chapter "The Uncolonized Mind". In spite of his English schooling and education in India and higher education in Cambridge, London he refused to toe the British line for the highest civil service. He came back to India and taught in Baroda and Calcutta like a true patriotic Indian. No wonder, he dropped his middle name, 'Ackroyd' during his study in English. He wrote:

> I know my country as Mother. I offer her my devotions, my worship. If a monster sits upon her breast and prepares to suck her blood, what does her child do? Does he quietly sit down to his meal...or rush to her rescue? I know I have in me the power to accomplish the deliverance of my fallen country.... It is the power of knowledge, *Brahmatej* founded in *Jnana*. This feeling is not new to me...with this feeling I was born...God has sent me to earth to do this work... (qtd. in Nandy 92).

Aurobindo's involvement in the freedom movement of our country landed him in trouble. For his politics, he was taken a prisoner and sent to Alipore jail.

His years in jail became a turning point in his life. It is here Nandy says:

> His year in jail, particularly the time spent in solitary confinement, made a great difference to him spiritually. He practiced yoga, read the *Gita* and the *Upanisads*, spoke to Vivekananda over the barriers of death and even saw Lord Krishna in the jail. Once in a while he broke the monotony by levitating. Even the graces for which he was most thankful were once he found in fail in 1908: 'the silence' and the 'emptiness'. From then onwards, 'whatever else came, came in the emptiness', and he 'could at any time withdraw from activity into the pure silent peace' (93).

Sri Aurobindo was acquitted of all the charges in May 1909 and in 1910 he received orders 'from above' (should we say divine order?) and accordingly he proceeded to Pondicherry, then a French Colony.

Sri Aurobindo met Mira Paul Richard in 1914. Nandy writes:

> Mira Paul Richard, at that time an attractive French woman of thirty-seven, joined Aurobindo, leaving behind her home, husband and children. Aurobindo and Mira had known each other through yoga before they actually met; they had been working together since the dawn of history to carry on the human evolution. (Though their joint work had spanned centuries, they still differed in style: Aurobindo made all his claims part-metaphorically; Mira more literally. Even in occult matters she was more down to earth.) Appropriately enough, she soon took over the organization of the Ashram and was given the title Sri Ma, the Mother by Aurobindo (94).

Sri Aurobindo became a Yogi and renounced the world. His supra mind could not be colonized—colonialism and post-colonialism did not matter to him. Sri Ma became his driving spiritual force. He achieved divinity through her—neither the West nor the East mattered to him. He has gone beyond the human world.

Leaving aside his revolutionary life he took to spiritual as well as literary activities. Yogi Sri Aurobindo's two immortal literary creations are *Savitri*, an epic and *The Future Poetry* (a piece of literary criticism). These two are free of the literary influences of British literature and criticism. For the first time in human history he made a woman 'Savitri' the protagonist of his epic of the same name. Moreover, his concept of the working of a poet's mind is based on innovative thought.

Finally, Nandy brings Gandhi to this text, "The Uncolonized Mind" to show what Gandhi noticed was not noticed by others. Nandy writes:

> Almost unwittingly I seem to have come back to Gandhi who was one of the few who successfully articulated in politics the consciousness which had remained untamed by British rule in India... Gandhi queered the pitch at two planes. He admitted that colonialism was a moral issue and took the battle to Kipling's home ground by judging colonialism by Christian values and declaring it to be an absolute evil. At the second plane he made his 'odd' cognitive assessment of the gains and losses from colonialism a part of his critique of modernity and found the British wanting in both ethics and rationality (100).

There is nothing moral about colonialism. It is an act of expediency on the part of the British to squander the wealth of India, to colonize the Indian mind intellectually and finally to exploit Indians spiritually by alluring them to embrace Christianity through conversion. Gandhi called their bluff.

In the last Section (VI) of the Essay, Nandy as it were, gives a summary of what he understood by colonialism and post-colonialism. This is how he puts it:

> I have examined, under different rubrics, four sets of polarities which have informed most discourses on the East and the West in colonial and post-colonial times. These polarities are the universal versus the parochial, the material (or the realistic) versus the spiritual (or the unrealistic), the achievement (or the performing) versus the insane. I have also touched upon a fifth set which cuts across these four: a self-conscious, well-defined Indianness versus a fluid open self-definition. At one plane, I have tried to show that the two ends of these polarities meet if the central problem is coping with—or resistance to—oppression and not the scholarly understanding of a

> civilization. At another plane, I have tried to show that the parochial, the spiritual, the non-performing and the insane can sometimes turn out to be better versions of the universal, the realistic, the efficient and the Sane (112-13).

Nandy has not addressed the question, embedded in the title "The Uncolonized Mind", that is, how the mind of the people of British India remained 'uncolonized', when they were politically, socially and economically colonized. In retrospect, I feel it is the large chunk of English educated Indians, if not all, were colonized lock, stock and barrel. The British had not only colonized our education, administration, judiciary but also colonized our taste for what is good and what is bad. Only the saints like Sri Aurobindo and Gandhiji were free.

WORK CITED

Nandy, Ashis. *The Intimate Enemy: Loss and Recovery of Self Under Colonialism* incorporated in *Exiled at Home*, Delhi: Oxford University Press, 2005, 6th ed. Indian Paper Back, 2012.

5

Creating a Nationality: The Ramjanmabhumi Movement and Fear of the Self

This book is a collaborative work done by four persons: Ashis Nandy, Shikha Trivedi, Shail Mayaram and Achyut Yagnik. In the "Preface" they make two significant statements:

1. This study of communal violence is actually part of a series on ethnic conflicts.... Usually, the core concept in studies of religious fanaticism is fundamentalism, in studies of ethnicity, it is nationality (V).
2. This book being mainly written from the point of view of Hinduism, makes no attempt to balance its portrayal of Hindu nationalism by a discussion of Islamic revivalism or of the cynical Muslim leaders who played a significant role in the Ramjanmabhumi issue (VIII).

It seems that this book grew out of field study as is indicated in the statement, "we specially remember with a deep sense of gratitude the help given to us by the Chief Priest of Ramjanmabhumi temple, Laldas, who was murdered in 1993 when the book was in press" (X).

The book consists of six chapters. Chapter I states the location of the temple town of Ayodhya being "situated on the bank of the river Saryu, some six miles from the city of Faizabad in eastern Uttar Pradesh" (1). It is believed that it is the birth place of Lord Ram, an incarnation of Lord Vishnu. Traditionally, Hindus and Muslims lived in harmony. Indian Culture is an amalgam of different religious traditions. From the Mughal time the two communities maintained the social harmony, not withstanding the sporadic violence caused by the fanatics of both communities.

Let me quote a long paragraph from the text which states unambiguously the Hindu-Muslim brotherhood:

> Unlike the famous temples in some other Indian cities, Ayodhya temples are open to all—Hindus and non-Hindus, Brahmans and 'untouchables', believes and non-believers. There are at least two temples that have been constructed by Muslims. One of them is still managed by a Muslim. A fairly large number of temples, according to their priests, have benefited from land grants and tax exemptions given by Ayodhya's erstwhile Shia Nawabs and British rulers and some of the most famous temples have been built on land donated specifically show their visitors documents relating to land grants given by Muslim officials during the times of the Nawabs in return for rituals performed by the priests of the temples. Hanumangarhi, for instance, was built with the help of a land grant from Nawab Safdar Jang (1739-54) to the *mahant* or abbot of Nirvani *akhada*, Abhayramdas, and Khaki *akhada* was established on the basis of another land grant from Nawab Shuja-ud-Daulah. Peter van der Veer goes so far as to say that Ayodhya became an important pilgrimage centre in the eighteenth century not as a result of the removal of interference by the Nawabs but, on the contrary, as a result of the patronage of the court of the Nawabs. According to the belief of some local Hindus, the city of Ayodhya itself was gifted to one Darshan Singh by the Muslim Nawab of Lucknow to honour god Shankara. Some priests say that the city was given as a gift by the Emperor Babar to the Acharyas, a Vaishnava sect. And there is at least one instance when a Muslim philanthropist donated his all for the founding of a temple and lived the rest of his life on the food and apparel provided by the temple itself (2).

This brings to our mind Nehru's observation on Hindu-Muslim interaction and mutual appreciation in the following lines:

> During the Mughal period large number of Hindus wrote books in Persian which was the official court language.... At the same time Moslem scholars translated Sanskrit books into Persian and wrote in Hindi. Two of the best known Hindi poets are Malik Mohammad Jaisi who wrote *Padmavat* and Abdul Rahim Khankhana, a scholar in Arabic, Persian and Sanskrit and his Hindi poetry is of a high quality (*The Discovery of India* 209).

Despite religious differences, Hindus and Muslims were closer to each other culturally and ways of living. The authors of this book, *Creating a Nationality* have reinforced it in the following words:

> In such a culture, Ram might not have been a national hero, but he certainly was a cultural hero. Historian Bipin Chandra tells us that in parts of UP the standard greeting used by both Hindus and Muslims until 1920s was 'Jai Ramji' (Victory of Ram). We found that in Ayodhya, even till 1991, despite what had happened during the previous few years, the Muslims continued to use the salutation 'Jai Ramji Ki' or 'Jai Siya Ram' (Victory to Sita and Ram) (3-4).

The controversy between Militant Hindus and Militant Muslims began with regard to the site of the Babri Masjid of Ayodhya "where an ancient Ram temple built by Maharaja Vikramaditya had been desecrated and destroyed in 1528 by Mir Baqi, a noble in the Mughal Emperor Babar's Court" (5).

This book is foregrounded in the belief that within Babri Masjid there existed Ramjanmabhumi temple 'with its garbha griha, sanctum santorum', which needed to be excavated. Hence, the need for demolition of the Masjid gained moment. The final movement came on 6 December 1992. This is the history of the Ramjanmabhumi Movement. The matter went to the Supreme Court which finally decided after a long hearing and handed over the place of the demolished Masjid to the Hindus. History as we know is part fact and part fiction. It always remains open ended and calls for re-interpretation.

What's nationality? Its not created but assimilated. What Nehru said in his two learned books, *The Discovery of India*

(1946) and *An Autobiography* (1936) remains as guidelines. Nation is not created on the basis of religion. Nehru refuted Jinnah's claim of two nation theory on the basis of religion. Nehru said:

> What a nation is, it is difficult to define—To Jinnah, India consisted of two nations, Hindu and Muslim. Nehru said, "Why only two I do not know, for if nationality was based on religion, there were many nations in India" (*The Discovery of India* 392).

Nehru was right. India was and still is a nation of many religions—Hinduism, Islam, Buddhism, Jainism, Sikhism, Christianity, Zoroastrianism, etc. Then, how many nations we have on the basis of religion?

The tragedy of India is that there is a perennial conflict between Hindus and Muslims since the Moghul period. These two are the most populous communities in India. Muslims are not minorities in India. How can we say a religious community close to 20 crores minorities? That is, a travesty of truth. Before I move forward to analyse all the chapters of the book, *Creating a Nationality* I would like to put the record straight. Neither all the Hindus nor all the Muslims are communal. A section of both the communities unfortunately had and still have communal bias. They should be taken as exceptions—not the rule. Jawaharlal Nehru puts the record straight in his book, *An Autobiography*:

> That the Muslim organisations have shown themselves to be quite extraordinarily communal has been patent to everybody. The Mahasabha's communalism has not been so obvious, as it masquerades under a nationalist cloak (467).

The Ayodhya Movement was built on communal clashes—it has nothing to do with nationality much less the creation of it. As we are born into a language (we are not creators of language but users of it), so we are born into a nation. Nationality as a cultural concept, preceded 'nation' as a geographical region or territory, India existed as a nation much before it became a nation-state (western terminology) the latter acquired name for a country.

In "Bhishma Parva" of *The Mahabharata* Sanjay describes "Bharatvarsha" as follows:

> The country that Sanjay describes to Dhritarashtra is not an agglomerate of fragmented regions and warring tribes but a single, unified, integrated land. Ganga, Sindhu, Saraswati, Godavari, Narmada, Yamuna, Gomati, Kaveri and many other rivers flow through its territory. Its provinces include Kuru-Panchal, Kalinga, Vidarbha, Kashmir, Gandhar, Dravida, Kerala, Karnataka, Chola, Konkan, and Andhra. In this country both Aryans and non-Aryans live (Gupta and Gupta 29-30).
>
> Tagore's song, our National Anthem, "Jana Gana Mana…" reinforces the idea of Bharatvarsha along the lines described by Sanjay (Das 13).

Gayatri Chakravorty Spivak reinforces this idea in her book, *Nationalism and the Imagination* when she says, "I believe with Eric Hobsbawm that there is no nation before nationalism. But I do not locate nationalism as he does in the late eighteenth century" (13). She goes on to say, "West Bengal is my state, India is my nation" (17). Very true. The two epics of India *The Ramayana* and *The Mahabharata* telecast in 1980s and 1990s respectively captured the imagination of Indians irrespective of religious differences. For example, "The Lakshmana Rekha", the line Lakshman drew to forbid Sita to cross it (an ultimate warning of danger) which Sita in a momentary impulse to uphold Dharma transgressed to give alms to Ravana which landed her in trouble, has become a national myth. It may be mentioned here that to awake the national imagination during the corona virus pandemic recently *The Ramayana* and *The Mahabharata* were telecast in April-May 2020 by Doordarshan (DD Channel) and Indian nationals enjoyed viewing them all over the world. Gayatri Chakravorty Spivak has rightly stated that, "Nationalism is the product of a collective imagination constructed through rememoration" (39).

Eleven years before our independence Jawaharlal Nehru wrote in his autobiography in 1936:

> Nation may retain, and will retain for a long time much that is peculiar to them—language, habits, ways of thought, etc. but the machine age and science, with swift travel, constant

> supply of world news, radio, cinema, etc., will make them, more and more uniform (*An Autobiography* 469).

Gandhiji wrote in *Hind Swaraj*, "As time passes, the Nation is being forged. Nations are not formed in a day, the formation requires years" (42).

In Chapter II of the book, *Creating a Nationality*, Nandy, *et al.* have included two sections, "The Battle for the Birth Place" and "Contending Reactions". What is recorded in the first section was published in the newspapers of the time and also in the electronic media.

There are points and counter points about the perpetration of violence leading to the demolition of Babri Masjid. Temples in large numbers had also been demolished in our country but that was never made out to be an issue between two largest communities of this country. It is a fact that Hindus questioned other Hindus indulging in communal violence. They speak for the protection of the Muslims. But Muslims never questioned other Muslims openly indulging in violence against the Hindus. It is incorrect to say that it was B.J.P. which ignited the Ayodhya issue. Nandy *et al.* quoted Atal Behari Vajpayee former Prime Minister of India and Syed Shahabuddin, leader of the Babri Masjid Action Committee to put the record straight. Vajpayee said,

> It was not the BJP which made Ayodhya into a burning issue. It was the Congress which did that. It was they who allowed the *shilanyas* ceremony. It was Rajiv Gandhi who went to Faizabad to start his election campaign and he solicited votes on the promise of ushering in *Ramrajya* [literally the kingdom of Ram but, connotatively, an ideal polity]. The BJP had to respond to the situation (38).

Then referring to Syed Shahabuddin, Nandy *et al.* observed:

> This is one of the few issues on which Vajpayee and Syed Shahabuddin, the Janata Dal MP and leader of the Babri Masjid Action Committee, agree. The latter, as alert as Vajpayee to the politics of nationalities, said to us in an interview in October 1990: 'Rajiv Gandhi played his cards very badly. Mrs Gandhi from 1979 onwards indirectly helped the Hindu communal and chauvinistic forces. I

> don't say that she was communal in a strategic sense. But in her quest for power she could take help from Hindu communalism as a tactical measure. It was she who really reopened the Babri Masjid issue.... And of course, her son was the beneficiary. He inherited this. And in 1986 on February 1, when the lock was opened, there is no doubt in my mind that the order of the district judge of Faizabad was a contrived order. The entire scenario was written by the government. It was done as a matter of state policy. Thus a monster was raised which grew and grew and has come to the present stage (38-39).

Shahabuddin's observation could be taken as a matter of opinion. It was not Mrs. Gandhi but Rajiv Gandhi, who re-opened the Babri Masjid issue wittingly or unwittingly. But Vajpayee was right in his views, as he understood the root of the conflict thoroughly well.

The arguments for and against the Ramjanmabhumi Movement are dated, especially, so after the Supreme Court judgement on 9 November 2019. Now that the Ram temple would be built there the matter is finally set at rest.

In Chapter III (the title chapter of the book) Nandy *et al.* dismissed the concept of "Hindu Rastra" as utopian in nature. Here is the observation:

> Though the concept of Hindu *rashtra* was introduced in the middle of the nineteenth century and later systematized by the likes of Savarkar, the concept is culturally hollow; it is nothing more than the post-seventeenth-century European concepts of nationality and nation-state projected back into the Indian past; such a nation-state is expected in contemporary times to be controlled by modernized Hindus and inhabited by their likes. It is this modern content of Hindutva which explains part of the enthusiasm for the idea among urban, middle-class Indians and expatriate Indians in the first world; they see their secular interests as well as private hopes, anxieties, and fears well-reflected in the ideology (63).

Nandy *et al.* have given their opinion about the formation of a political party and its sister organizations by way of explaining the revival of the Hinduism.

The two sections in Chapter IV "Hindutva as a Savarna Purana", and "Violence and Survival", we find the politico-social picture of India, leading to Ramjanmabhumi Movement. There are references to L.K. Advani's Rath Yatra through Gujarat and Rajasthan and also his arrest in Bihar which are in public domain now. One thing emerges from it is that neither the entire Hindus as a community nor the entire Muslims were involved in the process. Ashis Nandy *et al.* are objective enough to record it. Here are two extracts from the book (one, on Vajpayee and another on the common man):

> From Gujarat Advani's chariot entered Banswara where Chief Minister Shekhawat and his cabinet went to receive it on 10 October. Shekhawat had been a strong critic of the Rath Yatra in private, like the party's well-known national leader, Atal Behari Vajpayee, an erstwhile foreign minister of India. Both were afraid that the Yatra would isolate the BJP politically and destroy its image as a responsible all-India party built assiduously over the previous fifteen years. But like Vajpayee, Shekhawat had to conform to the party line in public (133).

> Like Munnu Mia and many others in Ayodhya—and for that matter in the whole of Avadh—Shamshi spoke elegant, somewhat Sanskritized Urdu, generously sprinkled with both Urdu couplets and Avadhi sayings. Shamshi told us that the relationship between the Hindus and the Muslims had not been destroyed by the events of 1990-91. In fact, the relationship had reverted to its older form. For the ordinary people had already seen though the games of the politicians. As a result, inter-religious relationships were again becoming what they had been over the centuries. When specifically asked, he said that his shop, which had predominantly Hindu clients, did not lose any business. The temporary aberration during 1990-91 was brought about by the love that some politicians had for power and money.
>
> In other words, rightly or wrongly, Shamshi blames greedy politicians entirely for what happened in Ayodhya during 1990-91. 'We do not want to fight among ourselves, neither

> the Hindus nor the Muslims.' Outsiders have instigated the quarrel and they might still manage to damage the good relations between the two communities. Some of the politicians have amassed massive fortunes; they might still precipitate some crisis or other; just as in the late 1940s, one Mr Nayyar spoilt the cordial atmosphere by introducing icons of gods into the Babri Masjid, and as, in 1984, Rajiv Gandhi aggravated the conflict by unlocking the masjid.
>
> Shamshi seems convinced that the issue of the Babri Masjid has been wrongly posed. 'In our faith, you cannot read *namaz* at a masjid built on forcibly occupied land.' Though doubtful of the wisdom of the courts, Shamshi claims that the Muslims were willing to abide by the decision of the Court. He, however, adds: 'We are capable of offering major sacrifices; we are also capable of giving enormous amount of love.' Islam does not teach blood-letting; it teachers one to live in peace with one another. *'Atma saf, paramatma pas'* (If the heart is clean, God is close) (173-74).

Shamshi represents the common man in India who were above religious divide in the country.

Thus, common people belonging to both the communities in Ayodhya were initially not against one another for they lived there peacefully for ages. Shamshi understood it too well. It is the influence of outsiders that created bitterness. Nandy *et al.* have mentioned it in the following words:

> Ayodhya is *'pavitra'* (sacred) for both Hindus and Muslims. Muslims have 1,24,000 prophets. Hazrat Shis was one of them. He is buried at Ayodhya. 'Let God give understanding to both us and them.' This is not the kind of understanding the politicians arrive at, Shamshi adds. For them the basis of any understanding is: 'You worship money; we also worship money' (174).

With Chapter 6 (XI. "The Final Assault") came both the climax and the denouement. Nandy *et al.* have pointed out that within three months (i.e., from the beginning of September to the end of November 1992) more than 90 meetings were held between the delegations of both the communities. VHP and Babri Masjid Action Committee leaders came to the negotiating table but could not arrive at a solution. On 5 December 1992 one of the four authors of the book, *Creating a Nationality* met Atal Behari Vajpayee to find out what was going to come. Nandy *et al.* have stated,

> Atal Behari Vajpayee was subtler when speaking to one of us on the morning of December 5 at Lucknow. Asked if, given the large gathering of *karsevaks* at Ayodhya, he thought the Babri masjid would remain safe on 6 December, Vajpayee said, *'Asha hai, aur ashanka bhi'* (There are hopes, but also doubts) (188).

Then came 6 December 1992, which later became a turning point in the history of India in the twentieth century. As Nandy *et al.* have stated:

> On 6 December, minutes before the Babri Masjid was attacked by the *karsevaks*, Sadhvi Ritambhara in a brief conversation at the site used a similar 'double entendre'. Asked if she thought that the Allahabad High Court order would be violated that day, she replied, '*Karseva* will be performed like *karseva*. Whether there will be any violation or not, you will see later' (188).

Journalists have reported the incident in their own way as suited the policy of the newspaper they represented. There was no unanimity in the print media about the climax of the incident. It was the most unfortunate thing to happen after Gandhiji's assassination on 30 January 1948.

Between the final day of assault (6 December 1992) and the day of final judgement by the Supreme Court of India (9 November 2019) almost 27 years have passed to heal the wound. But the opinions continued to vary. As in 1992, so in 2019 some people started asking questions but refused to give in.

Let me cite a few reactions to the Supreme Court judgement to put the record straight. The Supreme Court has ordered:

> The Central Government *shall, within a period of three months from the date of this judgment*, formulate a scheme pursuant to the powers vested in it under Sections 6 and

> 7 of the Acquisition of Certain Area at Ayodhya Act 1993. The scheme shall envisage the setting up of trust with a Board of Trustees or any other appropriate body under Section 6. The scheme to be framed by the Central Government shall make necessary provisions in regard to the functioning of the trust or body including on matters relating to the management of the trust, the powers of the trustees *including the construction of a temple and all necessary, incidental and supplemental matters* (p. 926 of the Judgement qtd. in *Frontline* 6 December 2019: 12).

The Court has also directed the Central Government to allot five acres (Page 923 of Judgment 16) Muslims to build a Mosque somewhere in Ayodhya.

A.G. Noorani questions this judgment in saying, "what right, power and jurisdiction has the apex court of a secular state to direct the government to construct the house of worship of any community?" He conveniently forgets that the same apex court has also given 5 acres of land for the other community.

In an Editorial in *Frontline* (6 Dec. 2019), R. Vijaya Sankar says,

> The Babri Masjid demotion case was a key moment in history when the judiciary's intervention was necessary to strengthen the process of secularizing society. For the highest judiciary, unfortunately it is now an opportunity lost (13).

The apex court has exactly done that 'to strengthen the process of secularizing society' (as quoted above). Taking a look at the closing sentence of the Editorial, "The battle of ideas continues" one can't help saying, what a travesty of truth!

Irfan Habib, a noted historian questions the competence of the Supreme Court of India, when he says,

> The Supreme Court judges are not historians. From what I have read of their judgment, their weakness in this field is obvious. They appear to have had no realization that Ayodhya, then called Awadh, was an administrative centre—during the Mughal days, the headquarters of a large province—with

> a considerable Muslim population. The possibility of the Babri Masjid having had no Muslims to pray in it during Mughal times is a simple piece of judicial fancy (*Frontline* 6 December 2019: 23).

Surely, historians are not gods. They easily get divided on religious and ideological lines. Their competence, though is not in question—their motive is never beyond suspicion.

Coming to secularism, who is a secular person? The answer is not only simple but crystal clear. A person who speaks for one community—one community only, without bothering about other communities, is a communal person. But the person who speaks for all the communities irrespective of religious differences, is a secular person. The apex court of India asked the government to assuage the feelings of both the communities. There are vast number of people among the Hindus and also the Muslims who are secular—only a small number of people are communal.

The title of the book, *Creating a Nationality is a misnomer*. Because what the four authors state here are only reporting about Ramjanmabhumi and Babri Masjid conflict its antecedents and the fall out of the demolition of "the structure" (what is commonly referred to). Then the question arises what kind of 'nationality' was created or sought to be created? It may be recorded that after 9 November 2019 Supreme Court Judgment the dispute between two communities has been settled for good. Going by Shakespearean dictum, we should say, 'it is better as it is' and the rest is silence.

WORKS CITED

Das, Bijay Kumar. *Critical Essays on Research Methodology, Interdisciplinarity and Indian Literature*. Bareilly: Prakash Book Depot, 2017.

Gandhi, Mahatma. "Hind Swaraj". *Collected Works of Mahatma Gandhi,* Vol. X.

Gupta, R.K. and Priyalakshmi Gupta. "Towards a Concept of Indian Literature". *Indian Literature* 25: 5 (Sept.-Oct. 1982): 28-55.

Nandy, Ashis, *et al. Creating a Nationality, Exiled at Home*. Ashis Nandy. New Delhi: Oxford University Press, 2005 rpt. 2012.

Nehru, Jawaharlal. *An Autobiography* (1936). New Delhi: Jawaharlal Nehru Memorial Fund, 1989. Distributed by Oxford University Press.

——. *The Discovery of India* (1946). New Delhi: Jawaharlal Nehru Memorial Fund, 1999. Distributed by Oxford University Press.

Spivak, Gayatri Chakravorty. *Nationalism and the Imagination*. Calcutta: Seagull Books, 2015.

6
Conclusion

After discussing the three books, *At the Edge of Psychology, The Intimate Enemy* and *Creating a Nationality* incorporated in a single volume under the title, *Exiled at Home*, it is imperative on my part to say how far this volume is helpful as criticism to be used as a tool to evaluate literature—particularly fiction. This is not a book of literary criticism but a work of social criticism in the line of postcolonial criticism. The first of the three books mentioned above contains six essays on nineteenth century history and the plight of Indian women under the ignoble custom called 'Sati', "Woman versus womanliness in India" under the British rule, "Political Culture in India", "the Politics of the assassination of Gandhi", "Indira Gandhi and the Cultural Politics" and above all, "T.W. Adorno's Psychology of Fascism". The first two chapters are on the conditions of woman in British India. Nandy has rightly observed that, "No wonder all major social reforms and attempts at social change of the beginning of British rule have centered on woman and femininity. It is by protesting against or defying the traditional concepts of woman and womanhood that all Indian modernizers have made their point" (37).

The second book *The Intimate Enemy* in the trilogy, *Exiled at Home* deals with the psychology of colonialism and the uncolonized mind is a well-written book on colonialism and culture. Gandhi occupies a pivotal place in both the first two books. The third book, a collaborative work, *Creating a Nationality* is on and about nationalism in the midst of religious divide between two dominating communities in India. It is more a piece of journalistic writing and reporting as is done in the print media.

Going along with Benedict Anderson both Gayatri Chakravorty Spivak and Meenakshi Mukherjee contend that nation is a product of collective imagination, 'constructed through rememoration'. The question arises then that 'whose imagination'? The obvious answer would be the imagination of the people of a particular nation. In that case the idea of nation precedes process of imagination. Furthermore 'the nation' is not merely an imagination but an empirical reality for the people of a nation. Meenakshi Mukherjee has unwittingly stated it when she wrote, "A nation gets defined often by the twin processes of obliterating the differences within its boundary and emphasizing difference with whatever lies outside the border" (*Elusive Terrain* 169).

Nandy's forte lies in diving deep into the psychology of the mind of the people under the colonial rule. What happened and how it happened could be analysed in terms of historical reality but why it happened in the domain of psychology. Take the case of Gandhiji's assassination on 30 January 1948. No doubt, it is the greatest tragedy of post-independence India. It is not only a crime against the tallest of the Indians of the twentieth century but a crime against humanity at large. Paradoxically, it is the assassination that gave martyrdom to Gandhi. Had he died a natural death, he would have been forgotten just as a leader who struggled for India's independence. Nandy's insight dives deep into Gandhiji's assassination. Nandy puts forth a controversial claim:

> ...Godse was not a demented killer. Jawaharlal Nehru, soon after Gandhi's death, claimed that Godse did not know what he was doing. I contend that more than any other person Godse did know. He sensed with his entire being the threat Gandhi was to the traditional lifestyle and world view of India. K.P. Karunakaran, a political scientist who has worked on Gandhi for a number of years, once lamented that only two persons in India had correctly assessed the power of Gandhi: Godse, who killed him, and G.D. Birla, India's biggest business tycoon, who gave him unconditional financial support in pre-independence India and reaped its benefits in post-independence India. I am afraid, at least in this one instance, the political scientist

> is more right than the political functionary. Nehru was wrong. Godse did reveal a surprisingly acute sensitivity to the changing political-psychological climate in India, by killing Gandhi. I can only add that the heightened sensitivity of Godse reflected the latent awareness of dominant sections of the Indian society of what Gandhi was doing to them. In that sense, Godse's hand was forced by the real killers of Gandhi: the anxiety-ridden, insecure, traditional elite concentrated in the urbanized, educated, partly Westernized, tertiary sector whose meaning of life Gandhian politics was taking away. Gandhi often talked about the heartlessness of the Indian literati. He paid with his life for that awareness (*At the Edge of Psychology* 87).

In "Gandhi After Gandhi", Nandy quotes Godse's last words in the court, who said that he 'had committed patricide to save the nascent Indian State from an anti-modern political neophyte and a lunatic' (qtd. in Falk, Jahanbegloo and Vajpeyi 114). Gandhi was, it should be remembered, a lonely figure preceding a year of our independence. It is not wholly true that Jinnah alone with his Muslim League was successful in bringing the partition of the country. On the other hand, the Congress Party and its top leaders at that time in their hunger for power played into Jinnah's hands and agreed to the partition of the country. We should do well to remember that the British Government and its representative, the then Viceroy, Mountbatten was the key player in the disintegration of our country. Gandhi should not be blamed for what he had not done.

About Nandy's assessment of Indira Gandhi a lot can be said and also debated. Nandy writes:

> Thus, towards the end of Indira Gandhi's rule, every small economic gain or institutional change became a justification for all the humiliations and sufferings imposed on a large number of people—in a *reductio ad absurdum* of conservative Marxism. Only when such indignities became the lot of the Indian intelligentsia as a whole, only when she began to see them as comprador intellectuals of the First World, did it become obvious to many that

> the tables had been neatly turned. And gradually the ambivalent admiration of small sections of Indian and non-Indian intellectuals towards Indira Gandhi turned sour and became its flip-side: a torn, ambivalent hostility towards her (119).

Nandy brings out a comparison between the father, Jawaharlal Nehru and the daughter, Indira Gandhi. Nandy says that, "Unlike Jawaharlal Nehru who was simultaneously the official leader of the ruling party and the covert leader of the opposition, Mrs. Gandhi, long before she imposed her Emergency rule had managed to affirm convincingly that she was the sole depository of power in the country" (*At the Edge of Psychology* 120). It is female psychology that women tend to be authoritarian and ruthless when they assume power. Coming to father-daughter comparison, it could be said that Nehru was both loved and feared but Indira Gandhi was only feared by the people (except perhaps, in the aftermath of 1971 Bangladesh War, when she was deeply adored by the people of India). Nandy has briefly mentioned the Bangladesh War towards the end of the chapter which is not fair. If the imposition of Emergency on 25 June 1975 was a political blunder, showing the western world including the US their place during the Bangladesh War in 1971 was statesman like unparalleled in the world. Her misplaced trust in her son, Sanjay Gandhi brought her ignominy during and after emergency. But her decision to call for election 1977 is an indication of her love for democracy. It is an irony of fate that her misplaced trust in her bodyguards brought her end on 31 October 1984. All said and done, her political life remains an enigma with an interplay between good and evil which baffles our understanding.

In *The Intimate Enemy*, Nandy makes an attempt to interpret a literary text from the stand point of the tradition of dissent in India. The literary text in question is Michael Madhusudan Dutt (1824-73)'s Bengali epic *Meghanadvadh Kavya*. Here comes Nandy's observation:

> As is well known, *Meghanadvadh* retells the Ramayana, turning the traditionally sacred figures of Rama and Laksmana into weak-kneed, passive-aggressive, feminine

> villains and the demons Ravana and his son Meghnad into majestic, masculine, modern heroes. It interprets the encounter between Rama and Ravana as a political battle, with morality on the side of the demons. The epic ends with the venal gods defeating and killing the courageous, proud, achievement-oriented, competitive, efficient, technologically superior, 'sporting' demons symbolized by Meghnad (19).

Nandy errs against proportion when he says in the battle between Rama and Ravana, the morality is on the side of the latter. It is a travesty of truth. How can an epitome of evil, in spite of his vast learning and vedic knowledge be the symbol of morality? Nandy further states,

> *Meghanadvadh* represented a different concept of tragedy. Not only were the good and the evil clearly separated in the epic, according to well-defined ethical criteria, but evil finally triumphed. Traditionally the *raksasas* represented a demonic version of masculinity which was unfettered by dominant norms and traditions. Now aspects of this demonic masculinity were endorsed, for the Indians, by the new culture of colonialism (21).

Colonialism, undoubted affected the lifestyle of Indians, more particularly the English educated Indians. It succeeded in creating 'babuclass' (clerks) to run the British administration. But it has not changed Indian value system and for them Ravana and Meghnad (Indrajeet) always remained villains (evil incarnate). The epitome of virtue is Rama and his brother Lakshman. Rama has passed into the Indian conscious as a paragon of virtue and has been deified. What I emphasize is that colonialism has never succeeded in altering the Indian concept of morality—good and evil (gods and demons of our mythologies).

Nandy is unfair to Vinayak D. Savarkar and particularly to Subhas Chandra Bose, whose patriotism was beyond question.

If Gandhi represented the civic, righteous, and non-violent aspects of Indian politics, Subhas Bose stood for just and heroic aspects of Indian psyche. Both of them are complementary to each other. Both of them are secular and both of them paved the way for Indian independence. We will do well to remember that it was Subhas Bose who first addressed Mahatma Gandhi as the Father of the Nation.

The first two books in the trilogy, *Exiled at Home* are useful works in social sciences including psychology, which can be employed as a tool to analyse India's colonial past. Nandy has dived deep into the subjects mentioned in different essays in the first two books. Knowledge, imagination, and intellect are fused together to dissect the past for the benefit of the present. Intellect and courage of conviction are Nandy's forte. He has opened the door to the past for the readers to see the events that happened in the colonial past (British India) and guided them in a way to judge the historicism of the text and textuality of history. In a way, he resituates the text in the context, which is also the premise of new historicism propounded by Stephan Greenblatt in nineteen eighties.

But the last book, *Creating a Nationality* is more or less a piece of journalistic writing. As a I have mentioned in the previous chapter, the Supreme Court Judgement on 9 November 2019 has brought an end to the Ramjanmabhumi Movement and Babri Masjid dispute. In a number of articles including the editorial by eminent writers in *Frontline* (6 December 2019) the judgement has both been hailed and also questioned on both historical and technical grounds. The fact that the apex court judgment has applied balm to the long-standing wound of the people and sought to assuage their feelings is the only solution to maintain harmony in the country. The fact that the dissenters are given enough space both in the print media and also in the electronic media is proof enough to show that India is a vibrant country of secular democracy.

Finally, a word about Ashis Nandy as a social critic. That Nandy is 'a contrarian', having an independent mind of his own is an accepted fact. As a well-read person he has an inwardness with the works of Michel Foucault, Benedict Anderson, Ranajit Guha, Stuart Hall, Frantz Fanon, Edward Said, Gayatri Chakravorti Spivak, Partha Chatterjee, Homi K. Bhabha and above all, Mahatma Gandhi. In an introduction to the book,

Ashis Nandy: A Life in Dissent, edited by Ramin Jahanbegloo and Ananya Vajpeyi, Jahanbegloo writes:

> As a matter of fact, we can describe the life and works of Nandy as what Theodor Adorno calls a 'non-dominative difference'. This is the voice of an independent critic and a free thinker with a vast encyclopaedic knowledge, who speaks the truth to power. But it is also the ontological standpoint of a contemporary thinker who has transformed his sense of intellectual marginality into an eloquent perspective of dissent as a philosophical and political position. Nandy is among the last great intellectuals of our time who lives what he preaches and who preaches what he lives, and because of this he has the courage to live as an 'outsider'. As such, he has created a grammar of intellectual resistance which has become a mode of civic friendship (viii).

In an interview to Vajpeyi and Jahanbegloo, Nandy says, that he never writes only for 'an Indian public':

> Very clearly I write for Asian, African and Latin American audiences—for the Southern hemisphere, let's call it.... I have worked for years with Asian and African scholars, perhaps a little less with South American scholars. For more than twenty-five years, I regularly went to four South Asian countries—Bangladesh, Nepal, Pakistan, and Sri Lanka—and my intellectual collaborators mostly come from these countries. You can guess it from even from my references and footnotes. I have recently said in a lecture in Japan that if, following Benedict Anderson, a nation can be an imagined community, there is no reason why Asia cannot also be another kind of community with a distinct set of attributes. The same thing can be said about the Third World. We do not have to greedily occupy the empty space vacated by the countries that constituted the Second World. The number of skyscrapers or billionaires need not determine the hierarchy of countries and cultures (336-37).

This reveals his intellectual independence and also transcendence of nationality. Here is an example. In his recent essay titled, "Beyond Brutalization" he assets:

> It is certainly not an accident that the new global heroes who have entered the world stage during the last four decades are virtually all votaries of nonviolence and have shown a sharp sensitivity to the growing brutalization around them: Nelson Mandela, Aung Sang Su Kyi, and the Dalai Lama being the best known among them. On all of them falls the shadow of Mohandas Karamchand Gandhi, disowned by the ruling circles in his own country (Dallmayr and Demenchonok 67-75).

Ashis Nandy's writings are known for clarity, inwardness with the subjects of study and above all, impartiality-free of any kind of bias. Last but not the least, his writings show the interaction between individual and the society in the last two centuries under British colonialism and after (i.e., post-colonialism) in our country. *Exiled at Home* is a book of social criticism in the tradition of postcolonial criticism in India. It depicts three important things: Indian nationalism, impact of colonialism on Indian people and the communal conflict in India.

Social criticism is horizontal, it moves with the societal changes. It deals with both fact and fiction in analyzing social conflicts issuing out of gender discrimination (as in Sati Pratha), communal tension (as in "The Ramjanmabhumi Movement") and colonialism versus anti-colonial nationalism (as in "The Intimate Enemy"). Historical happenings are factual but the interpretation of them are subjective based on individual perception. Like doctors, the historians also differ because of personal and religious bias. Take for instance, The Tajmahal—a monument of love, a great-work of art, which commemorates an individual love, which turns out to be an epitome of universal love between lovers. Sahajahan immortalized Mumtaz by building this work of wonder in her memory. There could be another view. That is, a whimsical emperor squandered the wealth of the land to commemorate a personal sorrow. Which view is correct? It depends on the individual perception and inclination. That is the limitation of social criticism. It is always flexible and open ended.

Nandy has rightly understood the concepts of nation, nation-state in the light of social criticism. He says,

> Finally, there is a growing belief that the changing contours of Indian nationalism and the concept of nation-state have contributed heavily to the growth of communal hostilities in the country. This belief is sustained by the clear difference between the standardized concepts of nationalism and nation-state—which nineteenth century India borrowed from Europe and which, since 1947, its modernist elite has applied uncritically to all situations—and the traditional Indian concepts of allegiance to one's soil and the traditional view of the state as a protector of a social order that is expected to elicit different levels of allegiance from different sections of the people (*Creating a Nationality* 19).

The difference between Literary criticism and social criticism is loud and clear. Literary criticism is vertical in approach as it aims at diving deep into the text (textual analysis with all its tropes, metaphor, paradox, etc. and above all the foregrounding of the text in the context), whereas, social criticism deals with the factors that went into the making up the text (i.e., the social factors that are responsible for the creation of the text). It is in this sense that the hall mark of Ashis Nandy's criticism is the interrelationship between colonialism, and post-colonialism, on the one hand and culture and nationality on the other over a period of time.

WORKS CITED

Jahanbegloo, Ramin and Ananya Vajpeyi eds. *Ashis Nandy: A Life in Dissent*. New Delhi: Oxford University Press, 2018.

Mukherjee, Meenakshi. *Elusive Terrain: Culture and Literary Memory*. New Delhi: Oxford University Press, 2008.

Nandy, Ashis. *Exiled at Home*. New Delhi: Oxford University Press, 2005, Sixth Impression, 2012.

——. "Beyond Brutalization". *The Courage to Hope: World Beyond Global Disorder*. Cambridge: Cambridge Scholars Publishing, 2017, pp. 67-75. Edited by Fred Dallmayr and Edward Demenchonok.

Select Bibliography

Asad, Talal, ed. *Anthropology and the Colonial Encounter*. New York: Humanities Press, 1973.

Bannister, Robert. *Sociology and Scientism: The American Quest for Objectivity, 1880-1940*. Chapel Hill: University of North Carolina Press, 1987.

Barbalet, J.K. *Emotion, Social Theory and Social Structure: A Macrosociological Approach*. Cambridge: Cambridge University Press, 1998.

Bhabha, Homi K. *The Location of Culture*. London: Routledge, 2004, First Indian Reprint, 2019.

Bottomore, Tom. *Sociology: A Guide to Problems and Literature*, 3rd ed. London: Allen and Urwin, 1987.

Burton, Clare. *Subordination: Feminism and Social Theory*. Sydney: George Allen and Urwin, 1985.

Cain, P.I. and A.G. Hopkins. *British Imperialism: Innovation and Expansion, 1688-1914*. New York: Longman, 1993.

Chatterjee, Partha. *The Nation and its Fragments: Colonial and Postcolonial Histories*. Princeton: Princeton University Press, 1993.

Chaturvedi, Vinayak, ed. *Mapping Subaltern Studies and the Postcolonial*. London: Verso and New Left Review, 2000.

Connell, Raewyn. *Southern Theory: The Global Dynamics of Knowledge in Social Science* (South Asian Edition). Chennai: Allen and Unwin, 2008.

Coleman, James S. *Foundations of Social Theory*. Cambridge: Harvard University Press, 1990.

Das, Bijay Kumar. *Twentieth Century Literary Criticism*, 8th edn. New Delhi: Atlantic Publishers, 2018.

——. *Critical Essays on Postcolonial Literature*, 3rd edn. New Delhi: Atlantic Publishers, 2019.

Edgar, Andrew and Peter Sedgwick, eds. *Key Concepts in Cultural Theory*. London: Routledge, First Indian Reprint, 2004.

Fanon, Frantz (1955). *Studies in a Dying Colonialism*. Harmondsworth: Penguin, 1970.

Featherstone, Mike. *Undoing Culture: Globalization, Postmodernism and Identity*. London: Sage, 1995.

Friedman, Jonathan. *Cultural Identity and Global Process*. London: Sage, 1994.

Giddens, Anthony. *Capitalism and Modern Social Theory*. Cambridge: Cambridge University Press, 1971.

——. *Central Problems in Social Theory: Action, Structure and Contradiction in Social Analysis*. London: MacMillan, 1979.

Gokak, V.K. *India and World Culture*. New Delhi: Sahitya Akademi, 1972 rpt. 1994.

Guha, Ranajit and Gayatri Chakravorty Spivak, eds. *Selected Subaltern Studies*. New York: Oxford University Press, 1988.

Hall, Gary and Clare Birchall, eds. *New Cultural Studies*. Hyderabad: Orient Black Swan, 2009.

Husain, S. Abidi. *The National Culture of India*. New Delhi: National Book Trust, India 1978 rpt. 1991.

Johanbegloo, Ramin and Ananya Vajpeyi, eds. *Ashis Nandy: A Life in Disset*. New Delhi: Oxford University Press, 2018.

Loomba, Ania. *Colonialism/Postcolonialism*. London: Routledge, 1999.

Loomba, Ania *et al. Postcolonial Studies and Beyond*. Ranikhat: Permanent Black, 2005.

Ludden, David, ed. *Reading Subaltern Studies: Critical History, Contested Meaning and the Globalization of South Asia*. London: Anthem Press, 2003.

McLeod, John. *Beginning Postcolonialism*. New Delhi: Viva Books, 2011, rpt. 2013.

Merton, Robert K. (1949). *Social Theory and Social Structure*. 2nd edn. Glencoe, IL: The Free Press, 1957.

Mukherjee, Meenakshi. *Elusive Terrain: Culture and Literary Memory*. New Delhi: Oxford University Press, 2008.

Nandy, Ashis. *Exiled at Home*. New Delhi: Oxford University Press, 2005 rpt. 2012.

Robertson, Roland. *Globalization: Social Theory and Global Culture*. London: Sage, 1992.

Seidman, Steven. *Contested Knowledge: Social Theory in the Postmodern Era*. Cambridge: Blackwell, 1994.

Sorokin, Pitirim A. *Contemporary Sociological Theories*. New York: Harper Bros, 1928.

Spivak, Gayatri Chakravorty. *Nationalism and the Imagination*. Calcutta: Seagull Books, 2015.

Swingewood, Alan. *A Short History of Sociological Thought*. 3rd edn. Basingstoke: Palgrave, 2000.

Tomlison, John. *Globalization and Culture*. Cambridge: Polity Press, 1999.

Vohra, N.N. and Sabyasachi Bhattacharya, eds. *Looking Back: India in the Twentieth Century*, New Delhi: National Book Trust of India, 2002 rpt. 2011.

Appendix

The Making of Indian Culture and A Reading of Ashis Nandy's *The Intimate Enemy* as Social Criticism

The origin of culture is deeply rooted in the tradition of the nation dating back to the pre-historic period. The making (should we say the development?) of culture can be found in the 'archaeological record' in the museum, worth the name. This record is neither a full report on Indian culture nor its authenticity is beyond question. Many things about the past are open to question because they are based on heresy. Normally people have believed in what other people (may be elders) have said about their country leading to the creation of 'factoids'. In *Myths of the Archaic State: Evolution of the Earliest States, Cities and Civilizations* (2005). N. Yoffee states that, "a factoids is a speculation or guess that has been repeated so often that it is eventually taken for hard fact" (qtd. in Kenoyer 41).

Culture lies in insignificant things which go unnoticed in ordinary times. But when the occasion comes their significance is noticed by the people of the land. For example, no religious function—be it house warming, marriage, sacred thread ceremony, even funeral rites can be performed in any Hindu House from Kashmir to Kanya Kumari in the absence of the Ganga water. Water is the generic force and hence, rivers are sacred to us. In the Indian culture, the country is the motherland (not the fatherland) the river is the Mother (Ganga Mata, i.e., the river Ganges), the Himalayas are also worshipped as mother. "Bande

Matram" Hail to the Mother is ingrained in our culture. Culture is a unifying force—not a divisive force like organized religion. After the death of renowned person his ashes are immersed in the river water as was done in case of Jawaharlal Nehru and now in August 2018 the same honour was given to Atal Behari Vajpayee when his ashes were being immersed in different rivers of the country. This is a social practice, we may say, social ethics.

In an essay, "Culture is Ordinary" (1958) Raymond Williams states clearly and unequivocally that, "culture is ordinary, that is the first fact". He goes on to explain how human society functions in the following words:

> Every human society has its own shape, its own purposes, its own meanings. Every human society expresses these, in institutions, and in arts and learning. The making of a society is the finding of common meanings and directions, and its growth is an active debate and amendment under the pressure of experience, contact, and discovery, writing themselves into the land. The growing society is there, yet it is also made and remade in every individual mind. The making of a mind is, first, the slow learning of shapes, purposes, and meanings, so that work, observation and communication are possible. Then, second, but equal in importance, is the testing of these in experience, the making of new observations, comparisons, and meanings. A culture has two aspects: the known meanings and directions, which its members are trained to; the new observations and meanings, which are offered and tested. These are the ordinary processes of human societies and human minds, and we see through them the nature of a culture: that it is always both traditional and creative; that it is both the most ordinary common meanings and the finest individual meanings. We use the word culture in these two senses: to mean a whole way of life—the common meanings; to mean the arts and learning—the special processes of discovery and creative effort (Badminton and Thomas 83).

In order to understand culture, we have to distinguish it from civilization. Well-known anthropologists such as Weber and

MacGyver distinguished civilization from culture by "restricting civilization to science and technology and culture to philosophy, religion and the arts" (Gokak 1). Gokak opines that the word "culture" itself is a mid-19th century German word used in the sense anthropologists are using it today. In the sense of "becoming more cultured," the German word goes back to the end of the 18th Century (130).

Two seminal books, V.K. Gokak's *India and World Culture* (1972) and S. Abid Husain's *The National Culture of India* (1978) make interesting studies of Indian culture from two different angles. Gokak studies culture in the context of society, politics, religion, secularism on the one hand and compares ancient Indian culture to modern Indian culture, Eastern culture to Western culture, on the other and above all, 'Indian Literature as an Expression of Indian Culture'. Abid Husain makes an interesting study of Indian culture period wise starting from Indus Valley Culture, Dravidian Culture, Aryan Vedic Culture, Vedic Hindu Culture, Buddhism, Jainism, Muslim Culture, Hindustani Culture and the impact of English Culture on India. Husain basically studies culture through history—his book is in a way, a diachronic study of Indian Culture. Husain said:

> The Dravidian Culture in South India and Vedic Culture of the Aryans in North-West India were in those days two streams flowing apart. But the time was near when the confluence of the two was to give birth to the first national culture of India (31).
>
> It is difficult to pinpoint as to when Indian culture and heritage came into being. In course of an article titled, "Our Cultural Heritage and Identity". Kapila Vatsyayan writes: So the peak periods of Indian cultural heritage which we learn about from history books and from many books on art history, especially Vincent Smith, list the cultural heritage of India as starting first from Sanchi, then Mathura. The excellence of Gupta art was reluctantly conceded, nothing else (Vohra and Bhattacharya 332).

It is certain that Indian culture began in Vedic Age and through the puranic age it reached the Mohenjodaro-Harappan Civilization.

Indian culture is reverential unlike the western culture which is formal. *The Ramayana* and *The Mahabharata* unfold before us this reverential culture. In this kind of indigenous culture, the elders are respected and their names are not taken in their presence. It is through behaviour that the culture of the land is reflected. The elders are reverential even to their peers as we find in *The Mahabharata*.

Culture is manifest in language, may be in a dialect. Gayatri Chakravorty Spivak in an address made at a conference on cultural value at Birkbeck College, the University of London on 16 July 1988 stated that, "the feeling of cultural identity almost always presupposes a language. In that sense, I suppose I feel a Bengali". Culture lies with the common people in the villages. Jawaharlal Nehru spoke of the cultural background which influenced the masses of our country. "Illiterate villagers would know hundreds of verses by heart and their conversations would be full of references to them or to some story with a moral enshrined in some old classic" (*The Discovery of India* 67). Kapila Vatsyayan corroborates Nehru by saying that when she interviewed ten Kathakali masters in Kerala, she found that all of them came from one village. The same is with Manipuri, Uripok, Saraikela, Mayurbhanj where culture lies with the villagers. Vatsyayan made a valid observation in the following lines:

> These were the village societies producing the culture that we are exhibiting in our metropolises...our cities themselves are a conglomeration of villages. Peel an Indian and a village will come out. First the region will come out, then the village will come out. An even if we all have a universal cosmopolitan identity, it is still a gasping village that will come out (Vohra and Bhattacharya 334).

The best example of our culture in the form of dance is seen in our Republic Day parades, unfolding before us the variety and the diversity of our culture merging into a unity called Indian Culture.

Culture is interconnected, cutting across provincial boundaries. Various dance forms like Odisi, Kathakali, Manipuri, etc. are not confined to the boundaries of respective States. Similarly, people belonging to purohit caste and profession cutting across provinces such as Bihari and U.P. Brahmins had their kith and kin in Odisha. Such is the case with Kshatriyas (warrior class) who had their kith and kin in other provinces. The raj families are married to people outside the state who belong to their caste and clans. Rituals are integral part of culture. All the sections of people in the society observe rituals and through them they get connected with each other.

Two statements recorded in the early part of this paper (Raymond William's "Culture is Ordinary" and my own, "Culture lies in insignificant things") reinforce the idea that culture is the common pursuit of mankind and it has nothing to do with formal education (i.e., university degree). People imbibe the culture of the land to which they belong if they understand the tradition and rituals of the society. Semi-literate persons who have mastered other art forms like dance, pala (that is, the rendering of the songs by six persons in a group through their performance on stage) know the nuances of language (particularly the articulation of words) better than the so-called university degree holders.

Kapila Vatsyayan's example of her teacher, Guru Amobi Singh from Manipur in a way reinforces my point of view. She writes:

> In demographical terms, in statistical terms he was a semi-literate. In cultural terms he was the greatest guru and also the guru of Uday Shankar...he said, 'All right, Kapila, now please read *Yogvahishth*.' The arrogant educated Indian in me said, 'Well, this man has taught me Manipuri for years and years. Now I'll read it out to him. What is the problem?' At one point he shouted and said, 'Stop, *Mago shabda ke aghat diyo na*', he said to me in Bangla. So I said, 'Guruji, what's the problem?' He said, '*Ashuddh path kar rahi ho*.' I thought to myself, semi-literate man knows his dance, etc., knows Vaisnava, Bhakti, Chaitanya alright but I am the great Vasuda Sharan Aggarwal's disciple of Sanskrit. But he insisted, '*Ashuddh hai, iska path nahi hoga*.' There was curiosity in me and there was faith in that man. I went to five libraries and checked the published versions. And finally I went through an original manuscript.

> He was right. I was totally wrong, yet, in statistical terms he was a semi-literate and I was highly educated. And it is these experiences which have given me eyes... (Vohra and Bhattacharya 348).

Indian culture is like a multifarious rose made up of various shades of colour emanating from the people of diverse faiths, colours, and regions of our country. It is plural—not singular and has a unity in diversity. It is secular—not communal and is integrated with Indian nationalism marked by the peaceful coexistence of various faiths in India—notwithstanding the occasional communal outbursts due to extraneous reasons.

II

The Intimate Enemy with a subtitle, "Loss and Recovery of Self Under Colonialism" appeared in 1983. Here, Nandy examines the consequences of colonialism and its impact on the colonized people. This book, "takes the idea of psychological resistance to colonialism seriously", says Nandy and further states that, "colonialism is also a psychological state rooted in earlier forms of social consciousness in both the colonizers and the colonized" (2). This book contains two parts: one, "The Psychology of Colonialism" and two "The Uncolonized Mind".

In Part I, Nandy discusses the relationship between the colonizer and the colonized stating that not only they act upon one another but there are reversible reactions between them: on the one hand, there are Indian anti-colonial nationalists like Swami Vivekananda, Iswar Chandra Vidyasagar, Raja Ram Mohun Roy, Subhash Chandra Bose, Vinayak D. Savarkar and above all Mahatma Gandhi and on the other hand, the critics of colonialism Rudyard Kipling, George Orwell and the British sympathizers of India's cause, Sister Nivedita, Annie Besant, Mira Behn and C.F. Andrews.

The imperialist view downgraded the Colonial India by placing it alongside the India of the past (i.e., ancient India). Nandy writes:

> The colonial ideology handled the problem in two mutually inconsistent ways. Firstly, it postulated a clear disjunction between India's past and its present. The civilized India was

> in the bygone past; now it was dead and 'museumized'. The present India, the argument went, was only nominally related to its history; it was India only to the extent it was senile, decrepit version of her once-youthful, creative self. As a popular myth would have it, Max Muller, for all his pioneering work in Indology and love for India, forbade his students to visit India; to him, the India that was living was not the true India and the India that was true had to be but dead (17).

The impact of colonialism on India is enormous. It is marked by 'economic exploitation', 'psychological uprooting' and 'cultural disruption' says Nandy. He comes down heavily on the colonialists:

> Behind all the rhetoric of the European intelligentsia on the evils of colonialism lay their unstated faith that the gains from colonialism to Europe, to the extent that they primarily involved material products, were real, and the losses, to the extent they involved social relations and psychological states, false (30).

The colonizer meaning the Britishers not only economically exploited India, but also imposed their laws, language, literature and culture on us. Apart from that they had a hidden agenda which surfaced in course of time. That is to impose their religion, Christianity on us by converting the Hindus into Christianity. Nandy rightly quotes the statements of Richard Congreve, Bishop of Oxford who once said, "God has entrusted India to us to hold it for Him, and we have no right to give it up" and What Lord John Russel, a future Prime Minister of Britain said about Africa applied to India, too. The aim of colonization, he declaimed was to encourage religious instruction and let the subjects "partake of the blessings of Christianity" (34). How clever are these two statements!

Let me draw a parallel between the British and the Moghul rulers—starting from Babur to Bahadur Shah Zafar. Babur invaded India and established Muslim rule. No doubt, there were some conversions from Hinduism to Islam but the Muslim rulers 'went native' (to use postcolonial term) and accepted India as their homeland. There were many inter-religious marriages between Hindus and Muslims without changing individual religions. For example, Akbar's Hindu queens were allowed to continue their faith and live like Hindus. That practice still continues in India. The best example is the Indian Film world in which there are many inter-religious marriages. The Moghul never colonized India and the native Indians. But the Britishers colonized us. The moment we achieved our Independence, they left for their homeland (i.e., England) except a few Anglo-Indians who chose to live in our country.

It is surprising to come across a small paragraph in *The Intimate Enemy* in which Nandy observes that, "Most Britons in India lived like Indians at home and in the office, wore Indian dress and observed Indian customs and religious practices. A large number of them married Indian women, offered puja to Indian gods and goddesses and lived in fear and awe of the magical powers of the Brahmans" (5). Is it so? Two pages after he makes another statement when he says that:

> The Raj saw Indians as crypto-barbarians who needed to further civilize themselves. It saw British rule as an agent of progress and as a mission. Many Indians in turn saw their salvation in becoming more like the British, in friendship or in enmity. (Nirad C. Chaudhuri, the latest example), which of the above two statements is true?

The intellectual class in India during the British Raj and even now got their minds tuned to British thought and values (whatever that may mean). As Nandy has rightly observed that, "the West is now everywhere, within the West, and outside, in structures and in minds" ("preface"). As a contrast to this the opposition to British colonialism and imperialism came from the leaders preceding Gandhi in the form of violent struggle to over-throw the British. In the words of Nandy:

> They sought to redeem the Indians' masculinity by defeating the British, often fighting against hopeless odds, to free the former once and for all from the historical memory of their own humiliating defeat in violent power-play and 'tough politics'. This gave a second-order legitimacy to what in

> the dominant culture of the colony had already become the final differentiate of manliness: aggression, achievement, control, competition and power (9).

Gandhi through his non-violent method, Satyagrahi (civil disobedience) gave a new direction and purpose to struggle against the British in order to achieve freedom. No wonder, Raewyn Connell calls Gandhi, 'the central figure' in *The Intimate Enemy*:

> Gandhi is the central figure in *The Intimate Enemy* and in Nandy's work as a whole. He is present not as the exemplar of any cultural or psychological pattern, but as the person who cracked the code of colonialism, who discovered the way out of dead-ends that had defeated all other Hindu reformers. He was the person who found 'the right state of mind' and made it not a secret defiance but a public ethic and a political program (*Southern Theory* 186).

As I have pointed out in the course of this paper, there were thinkers and well meaning intellectuals in Britain who espoused the cause of India against India. Nandy has rightly observed observed this in the following paragraph:

> Lastly, there was the numerically small but psychologically significant response of many who wholly opted out of their colonizing society and fought for the case of India. Some of them became marginal to the Western lifestyle in the course of their search for an alternative vision of an ideal society outside technocratic utopias and outside modernity. One may describe them as persons searching for a new utopia untouched by any Hobbesian dream. Such persons as Sister Nivedita, born Margaret Noble (1867-1911), Annie Besant (1847-1933) and Mira Behn, born Madeleine Slade (1892-1982), found in Indian versions of religiosity, knowledge and social intervention not merely a model of dissent against their own society, but also some protection for their search for new models of transcendence, a greater tolerance of androgyny, and a richer meaning as well as legitimacy for women's participation in social and political life (36).

Similarly there is an acknowledgement of gain from colonization in no uncertain terms. No doubt, the British economically, politically and psychologically exploited us but it is the British colonization that made us see into our own tradition and enriched our intellectual mind and world view. Nehru in his *Discovery of India* wrote that two Englands came to India, the England of Penal Code, imperialism and the England of 'Shakespeare and noble speech'. The imperial England went back but Shakespeare and English literature stayed back—it nourished our mind. English has become no less ours' than it primarily being an Englishman's. No wonder, Rajaji said, "English language is goddess Saraswati's gift to us". A.K. Ramanujan in course of an interview to A.L. Becker clarifies:

> English has distorted our traditions, but it has also made us look at our traditions. It is not enough to say that it is still colonialism and has done nothing but distort. This whole question of colonial distortion has been formulated in English. It requires a dialogue with English. English has been the 'other' through which we have returned to ourselves. English has become a part of us. To say we want to return to pre-English state is chimerical (*Uncollected Poems and Prose* 79).
>
> Ramanujan reverses the view point of the colonizer being 'the self' and the colonized being 'the other'.

Ashis Nandy corroborates this in a different language, when he says that 'no art, no literature, no science is entirely a product of one person. It is equally a product of one's times and location' (340). He further states that he writes not, only for, "an Indian Public, very clearly I write for Asian, African and Latin American audiences—for southern hemisphere..." (Jahanbegloo and Vajpeyi: 337).

In Part II, "The Uncolonized Mind" Nandy takes into consideration, India and the West from the stand point of post-colonial view of both the worlds. This chapter (i.e., Part II) is both the continuation of Part I and repetition of it. If Gandhi was given the pride of place in Part I as a central figure, Sri Aurobindo (1872-1950) takes centre stage in "The Uncolonized

Mind". Aurobindo's ancestry has been analysed with insight and precision in Section IV of *The Uncolonized Mind* from Sri Aurobindo's childhood to his study in England (the first part of the classical Tripos with a first class, at Cambridge University) and doing well in ICS examination but missing it for failing in the riding test—all these come in for close scrutiny in a couple of pages in Sections IV and V. Then came Sri Aurobindo (then Aurobindo Ghosh only after dropping his middle name 'Ackroyd', a western name given by his father) to India to become a teacher and a bureaucrat at Baroda and a revolutionary which landed him in jail. On being acquitted he moved to Pondicherry, a French Colony then. Then came the turning point in his life when he met Mira Paul Richard, "an attractive French woman of thirty seven", who left 'her home, husband and children' (Nandy 94), they were destined to be Sri Aurobindo, the Seer and Sri Ma, the Mother in later years. Sri Aurobindo's vision of Lord Krishna in Alipore Jail came true. He became a yogi, a divine power. Nandy is right in observing that, "it is impossible to read the life of Aurobindo without sensing the inner pain which went with imperialism in India" (Nandy 96).

"India is not non-West, it is India. Outside the small section of Indians who were once exposed to the full thrust of colonialism and are now hires to the colonial memory, the ordinary Indian has no reason to see himself as a counter player or an antithesis of the western man" (73). Far from truth, Every Indian felt the pinch of colonialism in their pulse and Gandhiji's tour all over India on rail and foot had ensured that. In 'every village there was a Gandhi' as Raja Rao has put it in his polite-religious Sthala-purana, *Kanthapura*.

Ashis Nandy's *Intimate Enemy* on colonialism both supplements Homi K. Bhabha and Gayatri Chakravorty Spivak what the latter two speak of on Indian culture and society ('Satipratha' and Subaltern) and finally, Indian nationalism which built up anti-colonial stand in our country. In a way, Nandy's work is also complementary to the much publicized works of Bhabha and Spivak as postcolonial criticism.

Finally, a word about the title of the book, *The Intimate Enemy*. The term is literally flawed because friends are said to be intimate—not enemies. We have expressions like 'intimate friends' and "sworn enemies". The title is 'ironical' and in a way, 'paradoxical'. That is because as I have said earlier in this paper, the relation between the colonizer and the colonized was bitter-sweet. I have quoted Nehru and Ramanujan in course of this paper to say that 'colonialism' had not only harmed us in the form of exploitation of various kinds—material, psychological, intellectual and cultural but it had united us, the Indians under the banner of anti-colonial struggle against the imperialists. Colonialism ushered in Modernism in India, and gave us the Indian Railways and Postal system which brought the natives closer. It gave us English language which helped us to fight against the British unitedly. Most of our illustrious freedom fighters—Gandhi, Nehru, Patel, Subhas Bose, Sri Aurobindo, Ambedkar and many others were educated abroad, who later on fought against the imperialist power. Similarly, writers, thinkers, philosophers such as Annie Besant, Sister Nivedita, Mira Behn, Rudyard Kipling, and many others supported our cause and our struggle the Independence. Thus, in a way our leaders knew their contemporaries in Britain well. Leaders and thinkers on both the sides of the colonizers and the colonized, though belonged the enemy camps, were intellectually closer to each other. It is in this sense we may take the title as paradoxical.

WORKS CITED

Connell, Raewyn. *Southern Theory*, Allen and Unwin, 2008.

Gokak, V.K. *India and World Culture*. Sahitya Akademi, 1972, Rpt. 1994.

Husain, S. Abidi. *The National Culture of India*. National Book Trust, India, 1978, Rpt. 1991.

Jahanbegloo, Ramin and Ananya Vajpeyi, editors. *Ashis Nandy: A Life in Dissent*. Oxford University Press, 2018.

Kenoyer, Jonathan Mark. "Cultures and Societies of the Indus Tradition", *India: Historical Beginnings and the Concept of the Aryan*, National Book Trust of India, 2006, pp. 41-97.

Nandy, Ashis. "The Intimate Enemy", *The Exiled at Home*, Oxford, 2005.

Nehru, Jawaharlal. *The Discovery of India*. Nehru Memorial Fund/ Oxford University Press, 1999.

Ramanujan, A.K. "Interview", *Uncollected Poems and Prose*, Edited by Molly Daniels—Ramanujan and Keith Harison, Oxford University Press, 2001, pp. 52-79.

Vatsyayan, Kapila. "Our Cultural Heritage and Identity". *Looking Back: India in the Twentieth Century*, Edited by N.N. Vohra and Sabyasachi Bhattacharya, National Book Trust, India, 2002.

Williams, Raymond. "Culture is Ordinary (1958)", *The Routledge Critical and Cultural Theory Reader*, Edited by Neil Badminton an Julia Thomas, Routledge, 2008/Indian Reprint, 2012, pp. 82-94.

Index